MOVING MEMORY

MOVING MEMORY

Remembering Palestine in
Postdictatorship Chile

Siri Schwabe

CORNELL UNIVERSITY PRESS   ITHACA AND LONDON

First published 2023 by Cornell University Press

Library of Congress Cataloging-in-Publication Data

Names: Schwabe, Siri, author.
Title: Moving memory : remembering Palestine in postdictatorship Chile / Siri Schwabe.
Description: Ithaca : Cornell University Press, 2023. | Includes bibliographical references and index.
Identifiers: LCCN 2022048192 (print) | LCCN 2022048193 (ebook) | ISBN 9781501769078 (hardcover) | ISBN 9781501770647 (paperback) | ISBN 9781501769085 (pdf) | ISBN 9781501769092 (epub)
Subjects: LCSH: Palestinian Arabs—Chile—Santiago—Social conditions. | Collective memory—Political aspects—Chile—Santiago. | Chile—Politics and government—1988– | Palestine—History.
Classification: LCC F3285.P35 S39 2023 (print) | LCC F3285.P35 (ebook) | DDC 983/.0049274—dc23/eng/20221220
LC record available at https://lccn.loc.gov/2022048192
LC ebook record available at https://lccn.loc.gov/2022048193

Contents

Acknowledgments

I owe a debt of gratitude to the many people who welcomed me into their lives in Santiago and without whom this book would have never come into existence. I first and foremost want to thank all of them—both those whose voices come through within this book and those whose presence lingers between the lines.

The bulk of the research for this book was made possible by the Marie Skłodowska-Curie Actions through the network Diasporic Constructions of Home and Belonging (CoHaB). The exchanges facilitated through this network have played a significant role in shaping my thinking and formed the basis of long-lasting ties of collegiality and friendship, for which I am grateful. At Stockholm University, I benefited greatly from the supervision of Erik Olsson, whose support and attentive feedback significantly improved my work. I also thank Shahram Khosravi for his encouragement and thoughtful input, as well as Annika Rabo, who offered insightful suggestions to an earlier draft. Many other colleagues—too many to list—made for inspiring conversation partners, offered helpful tips, and provided uplifting company in the lunchroom and elsewhere. I am particularly thankful for the supportive atmosphere generated by Tomas Cole, Camelia Dewan, Johanna Gullberg, Anna Gustafsson, Hege Høyer Leivestad, Johan Lindquist, Lina Lorentz, Ivana Maček, Hannah Pollack Sarnecki, Peter Skoglund, Isabella Strömberg, Susann Ullberg, and Helena Wulff. Additionally, I want to thank Tekalign Ayalew, Daniel Escobar, Tania González, and Andrew Mitchell for sharing all the ups and downs with me along the way. Fond memories of Heidi Moksnes and Anette Nyqvist will stay with me for a long time to come.

Carrie Benjamin and Špela Drnovšek Zorko have been treasured companions throughout the process of this research. The hours spent with Nydia A. Swaby discussing work and a million other things over the last decade have been among the best spent of my life. My warmest thanks to Parvathi Raman for her enthusiastic engagement with my work while at SOAS University of London, and to Helene Risør, Felipe Martínez, Juan Loera Gonzalez, and the rest of the anthropology staff for offering me an academic home at the Catholic University of Chile during my fieldwork. My thanks also to colleagues at the Space, Place, Mobility and Urban Studies (MOSPUS) research group at Roskilde University for their support and input. I am especially grateful to Mikkel Bille for his encouragement and commitment to supporting my research. Jonas Larsen read an earlier draft of the book and provided valuable feedback, for which I am thankful. I also extend my thanks to David Pinder, Anette Stenslund, and Nina Moesby Bennetsen for their support.

At Cornell University Press, Jim Lance quickly took an interest in this project and offered his much-appreciated enthusiasm and support—thank you. Thanks also to Clare Jones and the rest of the team. I remain immensely thankful to Stephen McEvoy for his support during the most crucial of times. Over the years, my work has been helped along by exchanges with a great number of people. Among these, I want to thank in particular Kholoud Al-Ajarma, Rachel Beaty, Avtar Brah, Juan Carlos Cruz Suárez, Nina Gren, Katie Horvath, Nefissa Naguib, Joshua Reno, and Andrés Rivarola, all of whom, in one way or another, played a part in pushing me in the right direction or keeping me on track at various points in the process. I also thank Agnete Plauborg Lorentzen for drawing the beautiful, illustrated map of Santiago that appears here.

Finally, I extend my most deep-felt gratitude to my family, by blood and by choice, mentioned and unmentioned. For making all the difference, thanks to Jeremy Payne-Frank. For just about everything, thanks to Lene Schwabe.

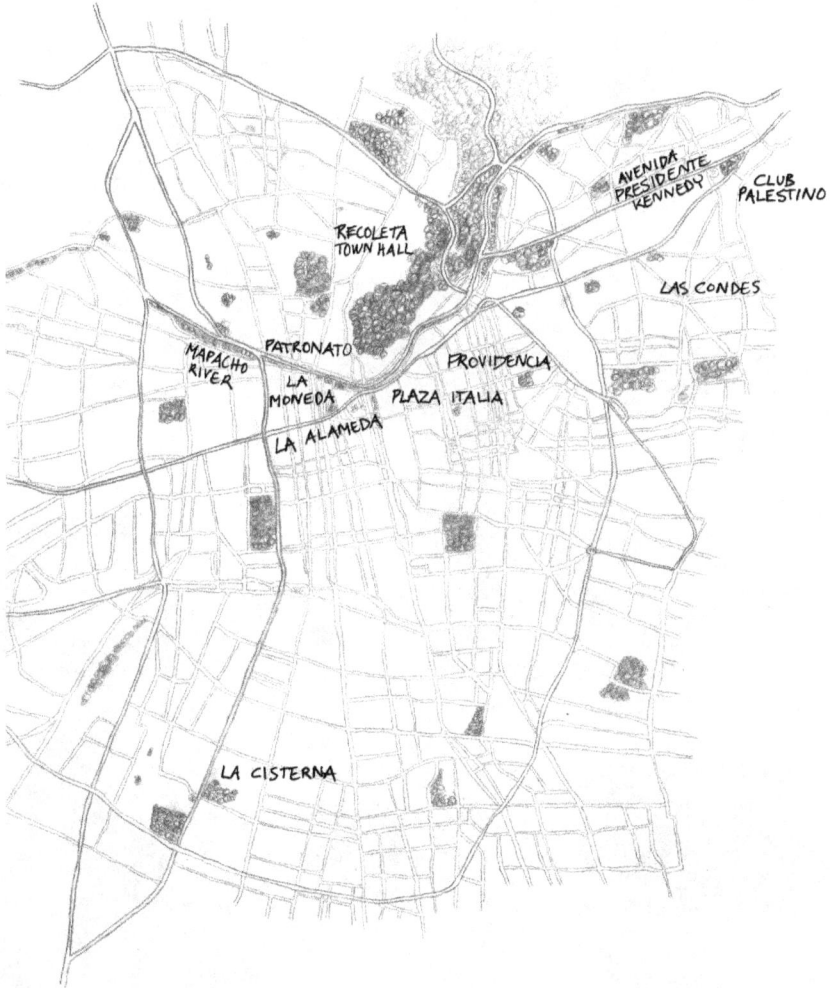

FIGURE 1. Santiago. Illustration by Agnete Plauborg Lorentzen.

SITUATING MEMORIES THAT MOVE

"¡Gaza resiste! ¡Palestina existe!" The chants resound along the ranks of roaring protesters moving slowly down the grand avenue of La Alameda in the very center of Santiago de Chile. Andrea, sunglasses on, moves along with the procession holding a sign that reads "me duele Gaza": Gaza pains me.[1] Next to the words written in black on white, a heart has been painted in the colors of the Palestinian flag. She is enclosed by the crowd, and above her head Palestinian flags are being waved, intermittently casting shadows on her face as she walks on. Andrea has been joined by many who share her Palestinian ancestry. Many of them are wearing reds and greens or sporting black-and-white keffiyehs wrapped around their shoulders or being swung around in the air as they move through the city making noise.[2] Meanwhile, behind Andrea, a group of indigenous Mapuche carry the colorful flags of their nation. A band of dancers and musicians performs for the marchers and the onlookers waiting at the side of the road or peering out through apartment windows. Ahead, a large number of red flags marks the presence of the Communist Party (Partido Comunista de Chile). Student groups carrying signs and banners promoting their union walk in front, and farther back, football supporters wearing matching jerseys beat drums and chant along with the protesters around them.

Although marches and political rallies are a common sight in downtown Santiago, this one was unlike most others. A couple of weeks earlier, Israel had launched the so-called Operation Protective Edge. Only the latest in a string of incursions into Gaza with euphemistic monikers provided by the Israeli military, Operation Protective Edge bore a name seemingly designed to indicate that

Israel was merely defending itself, much like 2012's so-called Operation Pillar of Defense. However, this fifty-day attack, which left twenty-one hundred dead, was subsequently analyzed as but another case of "mowing the lawn"—an expression that implies Israeli unwillingness to change the status quo via diplomatic means and rather keep Gaza and Hamas under siege and subdued.[3] The violence and destruction that played out during this time made news headlines across the world, yet continued for weeks despite the clamor of objections that surrounded it. As the description above indicated, the attack on Gaza did not go unnoticed in Santiago, and indeed, when news of Operation Protective Edge arrived, mobilization was both swift and substantial. Campaigns were initiated, debates organized, candles lit, and banners painted in support of the victims. Over and over, angered protesters gathered on the streets and plazas of the city demanding the Chilean government take an active stance against the violence playing out so far away.

Andrea and I had first met nine months prior to the Israeli onslaught, not long after my arrival in Santiago. I had come to the Chilean capital to conduct research on how Palestinian politics were practiced, experienced, and talked about in the context of diaspora. But as I had quickly learned, the connection to Palestine that people experienced here was most often not expressed in very spectacular ways, nor did it refer back to events as destructive as Operation Protective Edge. During the time I had already spent in Santiago, protests and other political demonstrations had been few and far between. While events like the 2014 Israeli invasion of Gaza spurred many people—and not just those of Palestinian heritage—to take to the streets in protest, researching politics in this setting had mainly become about studying the politicization of everyday activities. In the times between large-scale outbreaks of violence in Palestine and before Operation Protective Edge, supporting the so-called Palestinian cause had been about eating Palestinian food, dancing traditional dances, and nurturing familial ties. But at a more fundamental level, it had been about continuously commemorating the ongoing Palestinian struggle; in short, it had been about remembering Palestine and, in doing so, about what was often referred to as "keeping Palestine alive." This implied both an affective and a highly politicized engagement with memories transplanted from a drawn-out Palestinian past not lived and measures taken to negotiate this engagement under the fraught conditions of remembrance in the era of Chilean postdictatorship. As a result, my research came to center on the mnemonic field of tension between seemingly noncompatible memories that were nonetheless consistently confronted with each other in the spaces of the city.

The march for Gaza described above took place within a context where memory played, and continues to play, a multiplicity of roles. First, understandings of an unfinished Palestinian past marked by Israeli settler colonialism interplayed with a complex history of tyranny and dissent in the Chilean context to facilitate a border-transgressing yet highly localized string of protests. Second, these public demonstrations served in part to imprint on the landscape of the city reminders of pasts felt very much in the present. Over the course of two decades, from 1970 to 1990, Chile experienced massive societal change based around two pivotal and radical shifts: the first wrestled the country from the democratically elected socialist government led by Salvador Allende to dictatorship following a military coup; the second brought it back to democracy following the 1988 plebiscite to end the rule of General Augusto Pinochet and his junta. Since then, memory has remained a complicated issue and continues to be a sensitive and polarizing topic in a country where political fault lines are sharply drawn between *la derecha*, the conservative right wing, and *la izquierda*, the socialist left wing.

The presence of well-established Palestinian families, businesses, and institutions in this postdictatorship context only complicates matters of memory politics further. Not only are broader political divisions and diverging understandings of Chilean past and present reflected within what I call the Palestinian establishment in Santiago—the main diasporic organizations, institutions, and the people that actively align themselves with these—but this establishment also illuminates wider problematics related to the introduction of memories of a past lived elsewhere to a setting already marked by struggles of how to deal with the bygone.

Two central paradoxes spring from these circumstances: First, although most Palestinian Chilean families have been settled in South America for generations, with few Chileans of Palestinian descent having lived through the establishment of Israel in 1948 and subsequent waves of violence in Palestine, Andrea and many others consider "*la causa*"—the Palestinian cause—both much more present and more pressing than what could reasonably be considered more near at hand. Second, within a Chilean society marked by such stark ideological divisions, the Palestinian struggle has come to belong to both and neither *la derecha* and *la izquierda* at the same time. Some, like Andrea, frame the situation in Palestine as a continuation of a long, global history of imperialist and settler colonial projects that calls for a politics of solidarity. Others refuse such discourses and claim instead that they march and campaign for *la causa* simply because they feel *moved* to do so as Palestinians, albeit conservative ones with little or no expressed interest in other struggles. Not only do these circumstances challenge common perceptions of Palestinian diasporicity and politics; they also raise analytical questions regarding the relationship between politics, memory, and movement.

This book is about moving and being moved by memory, and about how acts of remembrance can both construct and dismantle barriers brought on by experiences of presence and absence, proximity and distance. I argue that the paradoxes presented above point to ongoing negotiations of memory within, across, and beyond both physical and imagined boundaries that echo wider dynamics of how we as humans relate to pasts and futures. To understand the intricacies of these negotiations, I employ the concept of *moving memory*: memory in movement within and between people and spaces. I use the term *moving* as both a verb and an adjective to denote both the mobile and affective aspects of remembrance and the interconnections between these. In order to understand these dual aspects, I approach the phenomenon of moving memory from a number of different angles in the chapters that follow. In chapters 1 and 2, I delve into the *content and context* of moving memory among Palestinian Chileans in Santiago. In chapter 2, I begin to home in on the *affective* qualities of moving memory and lay the foundation for a subsequent interrogation of memory's *absences* in chapter 3. Chapter 4 highlights how moving memory is *placed* and *bordered* within what I call *mnemonic landscapes*. In chapter 5, I open up an investigation into what happens when memory moves from discrete nooks within this sort of landscape and into the public spaces of the city and argue that memory borne by *movement*—in literal and figurative terms—is inherently unconfinable, despite efforts to the contrary.

In Santiago, Palestinian memory is continually confronted with incompatible, even opposing, understandings and expressions of what happened in the Chile of the not so distant past. In what remains of this book, then, I explore some of the tensions that exist between what might be called particular *bundles* (Maus 2015) of memories and the ways in which boundaries are constructed and contested at their fault lines. In looking at how memory is transferred from Palestine to Chile and is ultimately negotiated within a city marked in many ways by decades of state violence, political turmoil, and continued inequality, I interrogate the complexities of how memory moves—and sometimes fails to move—across and beyond physical and imagined boundaries. The boundaries I am concerned with are in part expressed and grounded in space but do not necessarily reveal themselves in the built environment. They are primarily products and producers of social life and are as such displayed in relations between people and institutions. These relations, in turn, are always placed but never quite stuck. This book, then, also deals with the (im)possibility of rendering memory immobile and confined. In many ways, I might add, the tense relationship between movement and stagnation is a central pivot around which the arguments presented here revolve.

I should note that defining the Zionist project as a settler colonial endeavor, as I do here, has certain implications. It works to subtly refocus views on the empirical reality of life in Palestine and Israel, but it also works to counter notions of Palestinian exceptionalism by drawing parallels to the continued effects of past and present colonialism in other parts of the world, including Chile (Salamanca et al. 2012; Sen 2020). Indeed, I hope the book will spark new ways of thinking about the role of memory as an affective as well as political phenomenon in the face of state violence and settler colonialism wherever these may be found.

Indeed, on a grander scale, this is also a book about (post)colonial connections and efforts to counter the conquest of both space and time, efforts that often play out at odds with one another. In that regard, this is the story of a particular web of ties forged across great distances and experienced in highly localized ways. With that, this is not an ethnography of *a* diaspora, nor is it a book about particular diasporic formations. Approaching politics of memory through the lens of diaspora is, however, illuminating of the border-transgressing entanglements between geopolitical projects and the pasts they draw strength from. Here, in line with Avtar Brah, "the concept of diaspora refers to *multi-locationality* within and across territorial, cultural and psychic boundaries" (1996, 194; italics in the original). Nothing is decidedly bound in that sense; rather, social life (in diaspora) is about a weaving together of social dynamics and practices that can entail connections to, in the present case, both Palestine and Chile. "The word diaspora often invokes the imagery of traumas of separation and dislocation," writes Brah, "but diasporas are also potentially the sites of hope and new beginnings. They are contested cultural and political terrains where individual and collective memories collide, reassemble and reconfigure" (1996, 190). It is in this way that I make use of the diasporic perspective: to shed light on contentious and ever-changing foundations upon which meaning is produced and from which new beginnings spring.[4]

Locating Palestine in Santiago

Downtown Santiago tells the tale of the city's past. In the part of the old city that lies between La Alameda,[5] the city's main thoroughfare, and the Mapocho River to the north, colonial-style architecture blends with large concrete edifices and impressive glass-and-metal high-rises. Between buildings, large buses and small cars make their way through the city via the wide boulevards and many small streets, imposing a net of constant traffic whose threads run past offices, shops, apartment buildings, museums, and landmark institutions. At Plaza de Armas, the old heart of the city, tourists can have their picture taken with a dressed-up llama or indulge in a taste of the local treat of *mote con huesillos*, a cool, sweet nectar served with wheat and peaches in large plastic cups. Meanwhile, locals pass through or pause on the benches by the fountain or along paths lined by palm trees. From this central square, surrounded by impressive constructions both old and new, the popular La Vega market is just a short walk away, as is the presidential palace of La Moneda.

Just north of downtown lies Patronato. An old district marked by narrow streets bustling with people and activity as well as an abundance of small shops, most of which specialize in clothing, Patronato was where many of the first Palestinian immigrants to the city settled down and set up businesses, stores, and small factories. Despite the changes that have occurred in the last few decades, with many of these businesses closing or moving out of the area, Patronato retains a distinct Palestinian feel, with numerous cafés, shops, and small restaurants still featuring the colors of the Palestinian flag and trading in shawarma, baklava, cardamom-infused coffee, and imported goods from the old land.[6] Other places add a Palestinian tint to the Santiago cityscape as well. Among them is the stadium called La Cisterna, located south of the city center in the district of the same name—a place well known to many Palestinian Chileans and others who support the local team: Club Deportivo Palestino, commonly referred to simply as Palestino or Tino-Tino. As the name implies, this team has a distinct connection with Palestine and the history of Palestinian migration and settlement in Chile, and the stadium itself bears the colors of the Palestinian flag: green, red, black, and white throughout.[7] More so than both Patronato and La Cisterna, however, the leafy compound of Club Palestino stands out as a particularly significant place for many of Santiago's Palestinian Chileans. Located on a large plot of land in the Las Condes district to the northeast of the city center, Club Palestino is a membership-based club that features a range of leisure facilities. As will become clear, Club Palestino became a fixture in my daily life during the time I spent in the city. Several organizations base their work at the club, and much of social life among Palestinian Chileans plays out there.

I spent close to a year, from September 2013 to August 2014, exploring these places and many others. During this time, I became involved with a number of Palestinian Chilean organizations, attended countless meetings and events, and spent time with dozens of people, only a few of whom will directly appear in the following chapters. Among the organizations based either formally or informally at Club Palestino was the local chapter of the General Union of Palestinian Students, which I will refer to in the remainder of this book as UGEP, a commonly used abbreviation for its Spanish name: Unión General de Estudiantes Palestinos. One of the most active and established among Santiago's Palestinian institutions, UGEP quickly became a focal point for my research, and meetings and informal gatherings with UGEP members soon turned into a big part of my every day. Many of the thoughts presented in this book consequently spring from interactions with the people who made up the UGEP core group during my time with the organization.

My research was not limited to the places and institutions already mentioned, however, but was carried out within various parts of the city as I moved along with the people and events depicted in this book. Especially during Operation Protective Edge, the streets and plazas of the city became venues for protests and spectacular happenings meant to cast light on the atrocities occurring in Palestine. On these occasions, people brought their commitment to Palestine and the Palestinian cause out beyond the realm of the Palestinian establishment, thus opening up new spaces for memory politics. Meanwhile, much of the fieldwork this book is based on took place in cafés, bars, and restaurants in central Santiago as well as in the districts of Providencia, Las Condes, and Vitacura, all to the northeast of the center and all relatively affluent. That it came to be this way has to do with two factors: that most of the people I worked with lived, studied, and worked in these areas, and that most events and meetings organized by Palestinian Chilean institutions took place within them. The fact that so much of my fieldwork ended up taking place in these fairly limited areas of the city has one implication in particular, namely that my research was conducted within zones that would for the most part be considered relatively upscale, meaning, in turn, that the people I came to know during my time in Santiago might, generally speaking, be considered relatively privileged. That this should be the case has of course more than anything to do with how Palestinian immigrants and their descendants have generally fared since their arrival to the Southern Cone.

Past Migrations

In present-day Santiago, a number of Palestinian Chilean institutions make up a network within which much of communal life is organized and lived. At the same time, there is nothing static or fixed about what I refer to as the Palestinian establishment in the city; rather, the social, political, and physical borders by which it defines itself are constantly challenged and changing. It does, however, spring from shared narratives of movement and settlement.

Palestinian migration to Santiago goes back more than a century, to when the first Christian Palestinians from Bethlehem and the surrounding villages of Beit Jala and Beit Sahour made their way across the world to lay the foundation for what has become a remarkable presence in the Chilean capital and beyond. Although a couple of people prompted me to conduct a census as part of my research, putting numbers on the Palestinian presence in Chile would be a challenging and not necessarily very fruitful task. What of those who have just one Palestinian parent—or those who have just one Palestinian grandparent? What of those who can trace their entire bloodline back to the village of Beit Jala but have spent years dissociating themselves from their Palestinian heritage? Exact numbers and statistics have very little bearing on the dynamics that characterize a daily life of remembering Palestine in Chile. Much more important are the practices, and indeed common narratives that interweave to form the texture of Palestinian Chilean social life. One of the most common narratives—and one that seems to have slipped into wide-reaching accounts of Chile's Palestinians— is that the Palestinian population in the country is so vast that it must be considered the largest outside the Arab world.

According to Cecilia Baeza (2014a), many of the Palestinians who first arrived in Chile crossed the Andes from Buenos Aires and São Paolo to avoid competition with already settled Syrian and Lebanese immigrants who were perceived as better organized. Most of these early Palestinian immigrants to the Southern Cone arrived in Chile from the 1880s onward, while others continued in other directions: to Peru, Bolivia, even Ecuador (Agar and Saffie 2005; Baeza 2014a). Indeed, some of the Palestinians who migrated around the turn of the twentieth century wound up in Central America, with Honduras and El Salvador becoming home to the most prominent Palestinian populations in the region (see Foroohar 2011; González 1992). As a result of compulsory military service in Ottoman-ruled Palestine, Palestinian emigration increased in the early decades of the twentieth century and continued beyond the world wars and the growing crisis in Palestine and what was to become Israel. Leading up to World War I, Christian families especially feared that their sons would be used as cannon fodder by the Muslim Ottomans (Arancibia Clavel, Arancibia Clavel, and Jara Hinojosa 2010, 48). Meanwhile, Muslim families who faced similar fears often did not have the means, social or economic, to send their young men abroad (see Baeza 2014a). Furthermore, the economic situation in Palestine deteriorated greatly in those years, inciting those with available resources to leave while they could (Baeza 2014a; see also Foroohar 2011). Significantly, very few women were among the first Palestinian immigrants to Chile. Those who eventually joined the men did so in their capacity as daughters or wives, at least in the early decades of migration (Baeza 2011).

With the Ottoman reign and the wars that transformed Palestinian life during the first part of the twentieth century, the migratory flows from Palestine to Chile from the late nineteenth century and for decades onward were largely colored by violence. At the same time, resources and the financial opportunities attributed to the emerging economies of the Americas played a large part in attracting great numbers of immigrants to the continent. Moreover, in the wake of the earliest migration across Europe and the Atlantic Ocean, familial connections became pivotal in motivating those left behind to make the arduous journey from Palestine to Chile. Knowing what to expect, and knowing they could find support from family and friends in this unknown territory, many more went on to take the leap from the old land to what would become their new home. For that same reason, most Palestinian Chileans today can trace their roots back to the area around Bethlehem and the nearby villages of Beit Sahour and, especially, Beit Jala, which are to this day Christian strongholds with close familial ties to Chile. Indeed, as Bård Helge Kårtveit (2014, 32) writes, in Bethlehem "the tales of emigrant success, and the vastness of the Bethlehem diaspora, especially in Chile, are retold with such regularity that they take on a performative quality . . . and emigration is elevated as the preferred and normal life choice among Bethlehem Christians."

As a result, much of the foundation for Palestinian life in Chile was laid in the years leading to the end of the Ottoman Empire, and Beit Jala remains among the most potent images of Palestine in Santiago—an image that invokes ties to Palestine, the Christian faith, and to a relatively wealthy segment of the Palestinian population. Indeed, while young Christian men were perhaps at a certain disadvantage as part of a religious minority in Ottoman Palestine, they certainly had advantages as emigrants; first, many had had access to education, mainly in missionary schools, and second, many came from urban families that were already established in trade and commerce—two factors both affording the young men with skills that would come in handy to make their new lives in the Americas (Foroohar 2011). Moreover, with Chile's large majority of Catholic Christians, both a hundred years ago and today, it is very likely that shared faith eased the process of settlement.[8]

At the same time, however, there were challenges involved in both the migration and settlement process, and what has been described as widespread discrimination against so-called *turcos* quickly ensued in Chile and elsewhere (see Baeza 2014a; Arancibia Clavel, Arancibia Clavel, and Jara Hinojosa 2010).[9] In Chile, it did not help that most Palestinians arrived at a time when political enthusiasm for immigration had largely subsided following decades of attempts to populate the country—attempts that, in any case, had favored European migrants (see Agar and Saffie 2005; Rebolledo Hernández 1994).

Despite these less than favorable circumstances, more and more Palestinians made their way to Chile during the first half of the twentieth century. While statistics are of limited relevance to what I explore in this book, it is worth noting that efforts to conduct a census were carried out following the first few decades of Palestinian and Arab immigration to Chile. In 1941, the *Guía social de la colonia árabe en Chile*, a "social guide to the Arab community," was published following sponsorship from Club Palestino (Mattar 1941).[10] A comprehensive list of names and, in some cases, background information, the *Guía social* comprised an overview of Chile's Arab population by order of location. In total, it featured 2,994 Arab families in Santiago, representing around 15,000 persons, including approximately 85 percent immigrants and 15 percent descendants. Of these, about

51 percent were of Palestinian origin, while 30 percent and 19 percent were of Syrian and Lebanese heritage respectively (Agar and Saffie 2005; Mattar 1941).[11]

Notwithstanding the relative privilege of those who were able to leave Palestine for the Americas, the story of early Palestinian immigration to Chile is one of hardship and poverty, but also, and importantly, a story of overcoming hardship and poverty through entrepreneurship and hard work. At the same time, there is no telling the story of Palestinian life in Chile without also taking into account two otherwise seemingly unconnected stories, namely that of continued Palestinian struggle and dispossession on the one hand, and that of Chilean politics and practices of state violence on the other. Both of these stories cast long shadows onto the everyday lives of the people depicted in this book, shadows that have much to reveal with regard to the entangled politics of memory in a world of sometimes unexpected connections. While the gradual displacement of Palestinians from Palestine has ebbed and flowed since the time leading up to the birth of the state of Israel in 1948, the story of Chilean state violence reached a crescendo during the era of dictatorship, which began in 1973 and lasted for almost two decades. During this time, Chile was irrevocably marked by the violent repression of dissent and a wide-reaching restructuring whose effects—both direct and indirect—can still be felt. While the junta imposed policies that directly opposed the initiatives of the Allende-led government it had overthrown, it upheld its own authority through the persecution, torture, and forced disappearances of those it deemed threatening. These circumstances have left Chile in a state of postdictatorship: a state in which military rule and its repercussions remain inescapable. Meanwhile, perceptions of this past and attitudes regarding how it should be handled still diverge and cause rifts in the social fabric, including within the Palestinian establishment.

The details of what these stories mean for Palestinian Chileans in present-day Santiago will be explored in much more detail in chapter 1. It is important to note here, however, that interlinking trajectories of migration, settlement, and simultaneous strife in Chile as well as in Palestine have played a great part in shaping the Palestinian politics on display in Santiago. This politics is, in turn, tightly bound to the dynamics of memory.

Moving Memory and Memory Politics

Memory shapes ways of seeing and understanding the world and, consequently, works as a foundation for ways to act within it. At the same time, practices of remembrance play a significant role in forming conceptualizations of past, present, and future alike. My approach to memory reflects the ethnographic grounding of this book and focuses therefore specifically on those aspects of remembrance that are practiced socially and relationally. Underlying this approach is the basic premise that memory is a social practice that works affectively, and that, specifically, it is the practice of making present. As pointed out by Michael Rothberg, "the notion of 'making present' has two important corollaries: first, that memory is a contemporary phenomenon, something that, while concerned with the past, happens in the present; and second, that memory is a form of work, working through, labor, or action" (2009, 3–4; see also Terdiman 1993; Fabian 2010, 19). With that, I do not dwell on differentiating between various modes of remembering (see, e.g., Fentress and Wickham 1992) but focus on the sort of memories that are worked with, through, and upon collectively, be it via narrative, commemoration, place-making, or other practices.

This approach likewise opens up to an understanding of memory and memory work as performative—that is, performed, acted out, and at the same time generative of new realities (see Cappelletto 2003; Johnson 2005; Wood 1999). Memories are in this perspective always both relational and inherently political, always products as much as producers of certain politics (see Boyarin 1994; Gillis 1994). That memory *works* means in part that it has an effect on those who interact with it. Importantly, however, this is equally the case in the reverse direction. Indeed, the term *memory work* implies a focus on how people engage with the past, ultimately shaping it, through remembrance (see, e.g., Gillis 1994; Hirsch 2008; Rothberg 2009; Stern 2010). Whether we look at memory through the lens of past events and experiences, or through present narratives and practice, activity, or work, it remains that the *then* and the *now* are entangled in ever-changing formations (Massey 1995, 187).

Fundamental to political mobilization among Palestinian Chileans like Andrea are knowledge of, and memories tied to, a traumatic Palestinian history that is continuously being written, with an ongoing period of colonial violence at its core. The past also remains a central element to contemporary studies of Palestine and Palestinianness (e.g., Davis 2011; Khalidi 2006; Khalili 2007; Sa'di and Abu-Lughod 2007; Slyomovics 1998; Swedenburg 2003). Notably, Edward Said (2000) has dedicated much attention to the importance of memory for the Palestinian people and the Palestinian struggle; indeed, his own autobiography (1999) must be considered part of his effort to recall and retell the Palestinian story. A common thread between these texts and others is the understanding that memory in the case of Palestine is always tied up in politics, always tied up in securing what Julie Peteet (2005, 21) has called "the right to a past that has an effect on the future" (see also J. Collins 2004).

Likewise, a complex relationship between politics and memory persists in postdictatorship Chile as much as within scholarship on the region. There is a vast literature on life after military rule, with much of it particularly focused on the dynamics of memory after dictatorship and efforts to reckon with the past through various kinds of more or less formal memory work (e.g., Frazier 2007; Gómez-Barris 2009; Han 2012; Hite, Collins, and Joignant 2013; Sorensen 2011; Stern 2010). As memory has become part and parcel of political transitions, understandings of the past have indeed become intrinsic to change (see Assmann and Shortt 2012). Further, as Katrien Klep (2012) has suggested, memory has arguably become "thicker" in postdictatorship Chile with every effort to negotiate and contest official narratives, and these efforts are still ongoing. Indeed, the past remains a concern in much of contemporary Latin America and beyond as nations grapple with the afterlife of the political ruptures and state violence of the twentieth century (see Jelin 2003; Shaw, Waldorf, and Hazan 2010).[12]

Within a setting influenced by both sets of contentious memories, what is most crucial for constituting and maintaining a shared politics among Palestinian Chileans in Santiago are not memories tied to a lived Chilean past, but rather memories tied to a physically remote past that overlaps with the present in Palestine. This facet of remembrance calls for an approach that acknowledges the importance of the passing of time but that highlights movement and foregrounds spatial configurations of memory rather than temporal. Building on both areas of memory scholarship, then, one of the main arguments presented in this book is that memory can be—and increasingly is—transferred as much through space as through time and relies on affective engagement in that regard. I consequently employ the term *moving memory* to denote both the affective and inherently mobile qualities of memory. Throughout the following chapters, I pay particular attention to the ways in which memories shift and move between both temporal and spatial realms and stir something in people along the way.

This approach is located in the slipstream of canonical works from within the transdisciplinary field of memory studies, from Maurice Halbwachs's (1992) notion of *collective memory* to Pierre Nora's (1989) *lieux de mémoire* and beyond. At the same time, my understanding of memory departs from well-established conceptualizations at critical junctures. Most significantly, I use Marianne Hirsch's notion of *postmemory* both as inspiration and as a springboard into new ways of conceptualizing memory. As a concept developed to grasp the experiences of the descendants of survivors, postmemory, in Hirsch's own words, "describes the relationship of the second generation to powerful, often traumatic, experiences that preceded their births but that were nevertheless transmitted to them so deeply as to seem to constitute memories in their own right" (2008, 103; see also Hirsch 1997). Like much of the foundational literature within memory studies, Hirsch's work grapples with Holocaust remembrance but has come to resonate far beyond it, not least in both Palestine and Chile, where intergenerational trauma continues to leave marks on families and communi-ties.[13] While a significant starting point for interrogating remembrance beyond direct, lived experience, the concept of postmemory does not fully encapsulate the dynamics of memory among Palestinian Chileans, many of whom—children and parents alike—have not directly experienced the sort of trauma Hirsch refers to. It is partly as a reaction to this that I develop the concept of moving memory and use it to provide an opening into the spatial, and spatially mobile, qualities of memory. Postmemory is defined by Hirsch (2008, 106) as "a structure of inter- and trans-generational transmission of traumatic knowledge and experience. It is a consequence of traumatic recall but (unlike post-traumatic stress disorder) at a generational remove." When Hirsch (2008, 111) suggests that "postmemorial work . . . strives to reactivate and reembody more distant . . . memorial structures by reinvesting them with resonant individual and familial forms of mediation and aesthetic expression," she by and large speaks to what is at stake here. The main difference between her observations and mine in relation to the present case, however, is that the distance alluded to is a distance primarily in space rather than time.

Paul Connerton (1989, 39) has claimed that "to study the social formation of memory is to study those acts of transfer that make remembering in common possible." In this case, I argue, those acts of transfer take place not exclusively at a generational remove, but at a spatial remove, namely from Palestine to Chile. Even further, memories are transferred between these two sites in the present; that is, memories are adopted by Palestinian Chileans from a mnemonic register that is neither lived by themselves nor their parents or grandparents.

My use of moving memory as a gathering concept throughout this book is likewise inspired by the work of Astrid Erll (2011) and can also be understood as a response to her call for an increased scholarly focus on "travelling memory" (see also De Cesari and Rigney 2014). By using the term *moving memory*, I seek to foreground and understand memories that pertain to an ongoing and liv-ing history elsewhere. Moving memory, then, is also memory in transit, con-tinuously transformed by and transformative of the processes through which it appears. Indeed, as I hope to show, a nuanced understanding of Palestinian Chilean memory in the context of postdictatorship Santiago requires thinking through moving memory as a form of remembrance that travels in space rather than merely in time.

Erll argues that, essentially, "memories do not hold still—on the contrary, they seem to be constituted first of all through movement" (2011, 11). In line with such a perception, rather than a study of "where memory dwells" (Gómez-Barris 2009), this is an exploration of where and how memory moves. Such an exploration is inevitably situated within and between particular places, but my central argument here is precisely that memory, unlike oblivion, is character-ized by movement and that this movement is reflected in both its travels and its tendency to stir something in people. From that it follows that the sort of memory I am concerned with here does more than travel. To me, approach-ing memory as moving implies an acknowledgment of the affective qualities of memory and taking seriously the ways in which memories work *on* people, often spurring them into action. In other words, in using the word *moving* I also want to point to the affective qualities that remembrance brings to bear on people. As will become clearer in the following pages, memory requires human effort to maintain its force but can conversely exert this force to mobilize people into action. In that sense, engaging with moving memory as an analytical concept is also to pay attention to the ways in which people are moved *by* memory. In both meanings, and as a social phenomenon, moving memory coexists with memories that, in contrast, appear static and unaffecting—memories that somehow fail to move and that, in turn, are kept still.

It follows that remembrance as the work of making present relies in part on practices of forgetting, making silent or invisible those pasts that might disturb or disrupt this work. Built into the labor of memory, then, is the labor of oblivion. Part of this labor, as I will return to in chapter 3, is focused on efforts to silence and render invisible those uncomfortable pasts that carry disruptive potentials, thus constructing boundaries that serve to occlude and ultimately make absent memories that leave people *unmoved* and intent on holding these memories still and at a distance (see Augé 2004; Connerton 2008; Lowenthal 1999). I follow Ann Laura Stoler in approaching occlusion as an "ongoing, malleable process" (2016, 14). The boundaries constructed in this process, I argue, never become entirely fixed. Rather, they are inherently porous and susceptible to constant de- and reconstruction.

"Our images of the past commonly serve to legitimate a present social order," writes Connerton (1989, 3). To that it might be added that certain meaning assigned to the past might work to legitimate the social orders of the future. To borrow from Karen Elizabeth Bishop (2014, 557), "the history at stake here is very much a future project."[14] At the same time, memories are always placed and prac-ticed within a certain era and, as such, are "historically conditioned" (Whitehead 2009, 4). Following from that, memory, as I understand it, always carries a certain openness, a potential to continuously redefine both what was, what is, and what will or might be as it "remains in permanent evolution" (Nora 1989, 8; also see Terdiman 1993; Tonkin 1992).

The forms of remembrance I deal with in the following chapters are never static or set in stone, and the representations they foster remain in flux. Although many attempts have been made within the present context to transform often repeated narratives of past events into widely accepted historical accounts, the past remains subject to change. In Chile, Palestine, and elsewhere, struggles over what is remembered and how it is remembered are ongoing, and form an important part of overarching struggles that go far beyond defining the past.

Across Mnemonic Landscapes

For the people I came to know in Santiago, references to the politics of place almost always implied references to Palestine as land and territory. Their political expression, however, was always tied to the (public) space of Santiago. Consequently, the connection between memory, space, and politics in this context is both marked by distance/absence and proximity/presence. In that regard, the approach presented here reflects a perception of space as fundamentally heterogeneous (see Foucault 1986) and—despite efforts to create borders within it—open (Corsín Jiménez 2003; Deleuze and Guattari [1988] 2004; Massey 1999, 2005). This openness relies on shared experiences of what is here and what is not. In other words, both narrated memories and mnemonic landscapes are organized around the juxtaposition of ever-changing presences and absences (see Bille, Hastrup, and Sørensen 2010; Runia 2006).

Indeed, absence is a premise for the work of moving Palestinian memory in this context; if there was no distance between Chile and Palestine, there would be much less need for memory to travel. In postdictatorship Chile, much of collective memory work likewise centers on what has been lost: family members or friends disappeared during dictatorship or, at a more general level, lost progress toward political or ideological goals—promised lands that somehow vanished along the way. For many of Santiago's Palestinian Chileans, however, a more pressing absence is that of Palestine itself, and it is this absence that, perhaps paradoxically, has come to make for such a powerful presence of the Palestinian in the Chilean capital.

While the boundaries constructed around memory politics do not necessarily result in spatial representations, space plays a particular role in facilitating them. Generally, as a social phenomenon, memory deals not only with time—that is, times past in the present and beyond—but is likewise grounded in space (see, e.g., Basso 1996; Conte 2015; Crang and Travlou 2001; Edensor 2005; Hoelscher and Alderman 2004). As Christopher Tilley (1994, 27) writes, all landscapes are embedded in memory; "their pasts as much as their spaces are crucially constitutive of their presents. Neither space nor time can be understood apart from social practices which serve to bind them together" (see also Bender 1993; Jones and Garde-Hansen 2012).

As a result, the divisions that are made throughout this book between the temporal and the spatial reflect little more than a forced compartmentalization, implemented primarily for the purpose of easing communication and aiding comprehension. Indeed, in "a lived world, spatial and temporal dimensions cannot be disentangled" (Munn 1992, 94), and the chapters that follow thus depart from an acknowledgment of the "intrinsic connectedness of temporal and spatial relationships" (Bakhtin 1981, 84; see also Massey 1999). My approach to space and place is thus inherently process-oriented (Low 2009) and allows for recognition of the multivocality of places, their pasts, and the people within them (Massey 1995).[15] Particularly in a context in which both spatial and temporal configurations are critical to a shared political project, it indeed becomes untenable to prioritize space over time or vice versa (see Dalsgaard and Nielsen 2015, 11; Massey 1999, 2011).

In both Palestine and Chile, remembrance is truly "part of the landscape" (Winter 1998, 1). In the former, memory and space are interconnected phenomena for particular reasons that pertain to the past as much as the present. There, land is fought over in a starkly uneven dispute, which has resulted, and continues to result, in the displacement of Palestinian people (see, e.g., Hanafi 2012; Pappé 2006). The importance of land to the Palestinian struggle—in the old land and abroad—can hardly be overestimated (see, e.g., Bowman 1988; Schulz 2003). Indeed, the threat of absolute disappearance of the land-as-Palestinian has served to politicize the maintenance of ties to that land and created a sense of urgency in always keeping the land present, even from far away (see Sayigh [1979] 2007).

As I will return to in chapter 4, it is not uncommon for Palestinian Chileans to experience a connection with the very land and soil of Palestine—a connection that often results in visceral reactions for those who manage to travel there and plant their own feet on Palestinian ground. "Our families would always talk about the past, and about their land, so that these things are impressed on the mind of a Palestinian child," a Palestinian refugee in Lebanon is quoted as telling Rosemary Sayigh during her fieldwork in the 1970s ([1979] 2007, 2). In the Santiago of half a century later, the past and the land remain shared focal points for Palestinian Chileans to whom Palestine is still front and center. The land and landscape of Palestine remain something to be remembered, cherished, and ultimately perhaps even returned to (Mason 2007; see also Barkan 2011; Gren 2015; Richter-Devroe 2013; Schulz 2003; Turki 1977 on return to Palestine).

In Chile, memory and land are likewise connected, but in different ways and under distinct circumstances. Unlike in Palestine, contested memories are in the Chilean context most often bound to a specific period of time, namely the years of military rule from 1973 to 1990. As something that belongs to an era long concluded—although its effects linger on—certain memories have materialized and thus make for a distinct presence within the landscape. In the Chilean capital as well as in other parts of the country, monuments, memorials, and places dedicated to memory often focus on ensuring a continued remembrance of, and indeed reckoning with, the atrocities committed during the dictatorship. Besides the memorials at Santiago General Cemetery (Meade 2001) and the Museum of Memory and Human Rights (Hite and Huguet 2016), Santiago features numerous sites designed for remembrance and commemoration (see also Hite 2012; Richard 2009). Some of these are former detention centers and sites of torture and execution, whose purposes during military rule have only been uncovered through a long and rigorous process of gathering victim testimonies and otherwise mapping the violence of dictatorship. Among these are Villa Grimaldi (Meade 2001; Taylor 2011), a suburban estate turned torture facility turned so-called "memory park," and Londres 38 in central Santiago, now a designated "space of memories" (*espacio de memorias*) (Klep 2013; Wyndham and Read 2012, 2014).[16] However, the transformation of these places into commemorative sites has been fraught with controversy and contention, and several others remain inaccessible as public sites of memory.[17]

Despite their importance in retaining memories of a troubled past, I am not particularly concerned here with the sort of places mentioned above. Rather, my concern is first and foremost with what I call *mnemonic landscapes*, formations constituted in interaction with diverse expressions and contestations over memory. In taking such an approach, I see both the fragmented Palestinian territories and Santiago as palimpsests, not unlike the postwar Berlin that Andreas Huyssen (2003, 84) describes: covered in vestiges, filled with remnants of the past and simultaneously revealing of attempts at erasure and oblivion. What characterizes these landscapes are years of unrest and violence, Palestine being at the center of an extensive settler colonial project, and Santiago having developed and changed immensely during the era of Chilean military rule and in the afterlife of dictatorship since the 1990s. How Palestinian Chilean memory politics fit into these landscapes will be explored most explicitly in chapters 4 and 5.

I approach mnemonic landscapes conceptually as dynamic fields whose particular formations all form parts of their whole; it is this whole, in turn, that I am especially interested in. Although much focus has been afforded to the role of commemorative memorials and official memory sites, both in Chile and elsewhere (see, e.g., Edkins 2003; Young 1993), my focus rests instead on those links between pastness and place that are more subtle. Mnemonic landscapes, like any other landscapes, are produced via processes that are "unpredictable, contradictory, full of small resistances and renegotiations" (Bender 2001, 4).

With that, I take mnemonic landscapes to exist beyond but never apart from the people who inhabit them (see Ingold 1993). As a particular realm—or space, if you will—this type of landscape is always "under construction" (Massey 2009, 17), always in the process of being produced, as is the city itself (see Lefebvre [1974] 1991; Watson 2006). Likewise, the meaning of such a landscape does not remain stable, either through time or across locations (see Till 2003, 290). With that, my focus on the spatial dynamics of memory largely relies on efforts to trace and contest past, present, and future through space (Bender 2001; Gray and Gómez-Barris 2010; Tilley 1994; Vergunst et al. 2012). Indeed, what is of particular interest here is the politics of geographical imaginations (Gregory 1994) and the spatialization of political imaginaries, both of which, in my understanding, are deeply rooted in the work of memory. Indeed, it might be added, "a landscape of memory is an imaginative geography" (Maus 2015, 218; see also Said 1978). In that regard, I follow Yael Navaro-Yashin's example in "conceptualizing the phantasmatic and the tangible in unison by privileging neither one nor the other" (2012, 5). At the same time, a focus on the imaginative also implies a focus on the transformative potential of the relations and actions embedded in mnemonic landscapes, and that indeed exists within the landscapes themselves.

TOGETHER APART

It is the height of summer. Everyone around us is dressed to an absolute minimum, and the asphalt, steaming hot, seems to be dissolving more and more with every passing minute. I am walking through Patronato with Laila, a young Palestinian Chilean woman. Her long, light-brown hair is kept up by an elastic tie, and her denim shorts and colorful T-shirt make her blend in perfectly with the young people passing us as we pause on the corner. Laila has offered to give me her personal guided tour of the neighborhood that has for decades been marked by a distinct Palestinian presence. By now, many of the Palestinian flags and signs with writing in Arabic have come down from the storefronts to make room for the more recently arrived East Asian immigrants and their shops.[1] A source of frustration—"It's all full of Koreans now," as Laila put it—these newcomers are thought by many to have played a key role in forcing out the hardworking Palestinian Chilean entrepreneurs. Indeed, their supposed disregard for quality and their connections to cheap Asian manufacturers are seen as making it virtually impossible for the old textile factories and clothing shops in the area to keep prices on par with the competition. Koreans or no Koreans, the fact remains that Patronato is no longer considered *the* home to Palestinian Chilean families and businesses. It does remain, however, a cultural and historical linchpin, a neighborhood full of familiar faces and affordable clothes, and a place where the smell of shawarma flowing along the narrow streets lends a fitting backdrop to a walk through the historical hub of Palestinian life in Santiago.

As we make our way past the small, crowded shops selling T-shirts, plastic hair accessories, cheap jewelry, sparkly dresses, school uniforms, kitchenware, and much more, the heat feels almost numbing. It is a Saturday afternoon, and visitors to the neighborhood have come out in large numbers to run their errands and perhaps have a fast-food lunch or enjoy a freshly pressed juice from one of the street vendors. Walking the cramped sidewalks feels like walking an obstacle course. Full of cracks and potholes, they are bordered on one side by shops with mannequins and clothes racks having made their way onto the pavement, sometimes accompanied by speakers blasting pop music and enthusiastic shop assistants chatting with passersby about the weather and the summer sale going on inside. On the other side, toward the road, the street vendors have set up their impressively large stalls. Row upon row of shirts and dresses reach back toward the cars, beyond and up toward the sky and just falling short of blocking the sun. The few openings that are left on street corners and in empty parking spots are taken up by middle-aged men and women selling melting chocolate bars and soft drinks out of Styrofoam coolers filled with ice cubes quickly turning into water. Laila stops me. "My grandfather owns basically this whole block," she tells me as she directs my eyes up to the brick building on the corner in front of us.

This chapter is intended to lay the contextual foundation for what follows in the rest of the book. It traces the Palestinian presence in Santiago—from the earliest days of immigration to current-day notions and practices of being Palestinian in Chile—and locates Palestinian Chilean practices and institutions within the field of tension between the still-unfolding Israeli occupation of Palestine and the continuing state of Chilean postdictatorship. In it I consider the fault lines that exist within and beyond what might be considered the Palestinian establishment in Santiago and begin to draw out the texture of what I call *moving memory*: the kind of memory that transcends distance as it moves across and beyond borders via dynamic processes of remembrance and oblivion that in turn display affective facets and have stark political implications. I show that boundary-making has a long and intricate history as a constituting factor in the Palestinian establishment in Santiago. In a broader sense, I argue that understandings of familial and communal heritage play a significant role in shaping a shared politics that centers on moving memory as well as the boundaries that are put up around it: that centers, in other words, on mobility and immobility both.

Moving with Memory

"My grandfather left Palestine on a boat as a child," Laila continues. "His mother took him and his four siblings to Italy, but they ran out of money." Laila looks enthusiastic but tells the story matter-of-factly, speaking loudly, with her voice adding a distinct layer to the buzz around us. "Then someone offered my great-grandmother work on a boat out of Italy, and she went, taking her husband and five children with her. The only money she had she used to buy jewelry, which she could sell in South America." At first, according to Laila, the family went to Bolivia, where a cousin was staying. But they decided to move on to Chile, where they had a larger network of relatives who had already made their way out of Palestine. When Laila's grandfather was eight years old, she explains, he thus arrived with his parents and siblings in a village on the Pacific coast close to the town of Viña del Mar, not far from Santiago.[2] From there, carrying their belongings in backpacks, the family set off walking inland toward the Chilean capital, where they settled in a small, rented room.

A sense of pride often permeates the narratives of hardworking Palestinian migrants and their descendants. As Andrea once said straightforwardly on the subject, "If a company has a Palestinian working for them, you know it's a good company." Andrea had herself been involved in many a business venture, as an independent entrepreneur as well as with family and within larger enterprises. Not all of these had succeeded, but the entrepreneurial spirit remained intact as she laid out to me her plans to expand her business endeavors to include one—or perhaps even several—shops online. If Patronato was no longer the right place to set up a new business, the world of online shopping was revealing itself as a promising venue for trade in the twenty-first century. And Andrea, having grown up surrounded by people who seemed to make their own luck, saw intriguing opportunities in online ventures.

Andrea was a fifty-year-old woman with curly brown hair whom I had met at a function at the Palestinian Embassy in Santiago's Las Condes district, hidden away between well-kept houses and blooming gardens in a quiet residential neighborhood. The yard behind the charming house had been decorated with small Palestinian flags hanging from a number of white marquees that had been set up to protect guests from the summer sun. Under these marquees, small groups of people sat around on plastic garden furniture, chatting, drinking soda, and eating shawarma from the grill or little pieces of homemade baklava that were on sale at a small table at the embassy wall. In the shade of a large Palestinian flag stretched out above the driveway, stands displaying Palestinian souvenirs and snacks for sale had been set up by the women's association that had organized the event, and the whole area buzzed with conversation and the rustling of wrapping paper as religious trinkets and little bags of sweets were prepared for the changing of hands.

While the eating, drinking, and small-talking continued around us, Andrea, who had taken the seat next to mine, introduced herself and almost immediately began telling me about her background. Stemming from a large family spread out across Chile, Andrea explained that she only sees her extended family once a year, when well over a hundred family members, from the oldest to the youngest, gather to celebrate the Chilean national holiday of *fiestas patrias* at the seaside.[3] Of Palestinian ancestry on both her maternal and paternal side, Andrea was deeply committed to her Palestinian heritage and to Palestine, but that commitment had begun wavering over the last few years on account of built-up frustration followed by a general lack of interest in the humdrum of social life among her Palestinian Chilean peers. She had not disengaged from her political commitment to Palestine entirely but had cut herself loose from conducting politics within the usual Palestinian Chilean institutions. Meanwhile, her understanding of her own Palestinianness in the context of Santiago remained clear and unabashed: "We are very respected here." "In Chile," she went on, "Palestinians are considered hard workers" and enjoy respect "as individuals, as families, as a community."[4] In Andrea's own case, being a hard worker was closely tied to the fact that, as she expressed it, she had always had a penchant for "selling things." As she explained, Andrea had therefore always done well in jobs rewarded by commission, where the effort she put in had a direct correlation to what she got back—assuming external factors were in her favor.

That Andrea by and large characterized herself as a salesperson, a merchant by trade no matter what was sold or where, seemed no great surprise. According to most accounts, the majority of Palestinians took up small-time vending when they arrived in Chile, such as was the case with Laila's great-grandparents and, later, grandfather. Although many Palestinians came to Chile in the first decades of the twentieth century, both of Laila's maternal grandparents arrived as children following the establishment of the state of Israel and the violence that followed in its wake. However, their story of migration and early days of settlement echoes that of earlier Palestinian newcomers to the South American continent, and in particular Chile. When her maternal grandmother arrived in Santiago, Laila told me, her parents began working where they could, trading exclusively in "small things" (*puro cosas chicas*), selling fruit and fixing houses, but always "working all day long." Meanwhile, her grandfather's family had started trading in wool and selling woolen garments after a stint of vending newspapers to save money to set up a proper business. Gradually, according to Laila, both sides of the family worked their way up, and Laila's grandparents succeeded in securing a comfortable life for their children, instilling in them the same entrepreneurial spirit that ensured them stability for life upon becoming settled in the Chilean capital. Andrea told me a very similar story about her own family on a later occasion. After her great-grandparents arrived in Chile from the Palestinian village of Beit Jala, they "started selling things, like handkerchiefs, combs, baskets" by the roadside, while keeping horses to carry the goods. "They didn't have a profession," as Andrea pointed out, "they just sold things," traveling from the south of Chile all the way to the mining towns in the north to do business.[5]

While most Palestinians, and indeed Arabs, started out as door-to-door vendors in Chile and throughout the continent, by the 1930s a Great Depression–induced political focus on import substitution meant that many were able to establish themselves in the industrial arena (Baeza 2014a).[6] The clothing and textile industry proved an especially prolific venue, and one that fit relatively well with earlier endeavors (see Winn 1986). The case of Andrea's father exemplifies the general move from vending to producing that took place among Palestinians and their descendants during that time. Before moving their family to Santiago, Andrea's father learned to make clothing, with "everything custom-made." After learning the trade, he opened a shop by the coast near Viña del Mar but did not stay long. As she related to me, Andrea's father died at a relatively young age after having relocated to Santiago, which left his wife to provide for the children. Andrea's mother, in turn, went on to work hard and became a successful tailor and clothing manufacturer herself. As Andrea expressed it, "She worked in Patronato when Patronato was nothing. It wasn't this big commercial conglomerate in the early 1970s. There were houses, and in the front of the houses somebody would open a store." It was only later, she explained, that "it began to flourish, it grew and grew, and it became much more well-known as a neighborhood."

Patronato still stands as a testament to the days when Palestinian textile businesses flourished, and the industrial look of concrete warehouses mixed with little shops and restaurants serving both workers and shoppers stands out in the Santiago of the new millennium, where much of the retail sector has grown bigger, faster, and shinier. At the same time, however, most Palestinian Chileans have moved up and out of Patronato. While both Laila and Andrea as well as many others remain attached to the place of earlier generations' settlement in Santiago, their daily lives are for the most part fairly removed, both geographically and otherwise, from the old neighborhood. A great part of the Palestinian Chileans whose families came into wealth during the heyday of Patronato now live farther away from the city center; the affluent Las Condes district to the northeast of downtown Santiago, in particular, has become home to many Palestinian Chilean families and institutions.

The Politics of Success

In his memoir, Said (1999, 3) points out that "all families invent their parents and children, give each of them a story, character, fate, and even a language." In Santiago, as Palestinian Chilean families continue to invent and reinvent themselves,

Palestine and Palestinianness is likewise reimagined and retold across generations. The family home and the intimate relationships between kin are unsurprisingly central to any comprehension of what being Palestinian means in the
particular setting of the Chilean capital, and how it comes to mean anything at
all. At the same time, the *stories* people tell about themselves and their families
act as crucial bearers and generators of meaning. Without a doubt, family narratives can function as double-edged swords: they consolidate or reconfigure the
characters of which they tell while they similarly position the teller according to
the told. When Andrea told me of the respect Palestinians and their descendants
enjoy in Chilean society, she spoke in general terms, all the while telling me the
story of herself as a hardworking and successful, indeed respected, entrepreneur.

The professional and financial success of many Palestinian Chileans in the
mid-twentieth century meant that the socialist Salvador Allende's rise to power
in the 1960s and his election as president in 1970 essentially posed a threat to
everything that had been gained through hard work in the decades prior. While
some had begun adopting socialist, even communist, politics, those who had succeeded in business and made their way into the higher rungs of Chilean society
by that time for the most part stuck to conservative values. When the Allende
administration, pressured by unions, began to nationalize industry in the early
1970s, textile plants belonging to several Palestinian families were seized, and
greater dissatisfaction unsurprisingly ensued (Baeza 2014a; see also Gómez-
Barris 2009; Paley 2001).[7] Subsequently, when Pinochet came into power following the military coup in 1973, factories were duly handed back to their previous
owners, but in the decades that followed the tumultuous 1970s, a large number of
Palestinian Chileans moved their business ventures into other arenas. Ironically,
as Baeza (2014a) points out, the neoliberal policies that came into play following
Pinochet's takeover ultimately caused the previously blooming textile industry
to whither as international competition was introduced to the Chilean playing
field. By then, however, many Palestinian Chileans had already formed strong ties
with the Chilean right wing and would remain loyal. As Andrea explained to me,

> Here in Chile, the Palestinian community was at first [made up of] very
> humble people, but they began to move up, and when the coup happened,
> Palestinians here had power. . . . Let's see, there was social and political
> reform, and right-wing people began to protect themselves financially
> because their properties were being seized. They saw that when the coup
> happened, *la derecha* protected private property, you understand? So,
> they attached themselves to the political right wing, and they remained
> protected by that man, by Pinochet and *la derecha*, because he protected

their economic interests. Two generations had passed [since the first Palestinian immigrants settled in Chile], and they had worked hard to get to where they were. And now they were losing everything, being left with nothing. So financially [the right wing] worked for them, they went for *la derecha*, and they stayed with *la derecha*.

This story was by no means uncommon among the Palestinian Chileans I talked to about the issue. By and large, through their business ventures the majority of Palestinians and their descendants in Chile seemed to have become indelibly tied to a capitalist framework, which was to culminate in the violent implementation of a staunch neoliberal agenda following the coup—and which has now become part and parcel of Chilean life far and wide (see Han 2012). For many younger Palestinian Chileans, growing up on the wealth of previous generations had allowed for greater freedom to pursue education, and at the time of my fieldwork fewer and fewer seemed interested in taking over the family business, opting rather for careers in business management, law, finance, journalism, or fields even further from those in which their parents worked. During my time in Santiago, most of the young people I spent time with were either studying at university or at the early stages of careers within precisely these fields. For instance, apart from being a relatively new but nonetheless very active member of UGEP, Laila, who was in her early twenties by the time we met, was also pursuing a degree in business.

During our walk, Laila talked at length about the neighborhood, and it was clear that she had become familiar with the place throughout a lifetime of walking, eating, chatting, shopping, and spending time with her grandfather and the rest of the family in all corners of it. Our tour was thus accompanied by stories of where Laila used to go to buy her school uniform, of who owned this or that shop, where the good places were for buying dresses and fancy purses, and how the neighborhood was always dominated by Palestinian businesses, institutions, and people. She greeted familiar passersby along the way, and several times I was pulled into shops to be introduced to the shopkeepers and then linger in the background while Laila exchanged the usual pleasantries with them before once more leading me outward and onward. Among these shopkeepers were her aunt, a designer and business-owner, and a friend's father who still runs a company producing and selling fabrics on the edge of Patronato. Under the hustle and bustle of the neighborhood, then, lay an undercurrent of intimacy. Several times during the day, Laila spoke very proudly of her family, and especially her illiterate grandfather who only learned to read and write at the age of fifty, motivated by his granddaughter who was then just starting to learn herself. When she pointed to the building on the corner and said that her grandfather "owns basically this whole block," Laila clarified that she meant that he owned the large gray building that was located there, including several shops that he was renting out while doing business from an office on the first floor. Like many others, she said, Laila's grandfather was now too old to care for working directly with the shops and had decided to let others take over the retail spaces below his office. Although Laila and her brothers sometimes tried to make themselves useful at his office, it seemed unlikely that any of them would keep the family business running, and there seemed to have been little interest from the middle generation, including from Laila's mother. Indeed, while a large proportion of the shops in Patronato are still owned by Palestinians, most have been rented out to Chileans of all kinds and backgrounds for their own businesses.

At the same time, the value of hard work is continuously emphasized from one generation of Palestinian Chileans to the next. Indeed, as she told me, Laila had previously taken on work in a Palestinian restaurant elsewhere in the city— if only for a couple of months—because she wanted to learn about "the value of money." She had always been given everything, she said, but she wanted to know what it was like to work. In the early days, so the story goes, Palestinian immigrants were treated poorly because they took up work that was considered low status. Later on, they were discriminated against because they had become successful—a fact that seemed hard to swallow for those who saw their position threatened, and perhaps even for those who had not been able to make the same kind of headway (see Baeza 2014a; Foroohar 2011). These dynamics, however, were and remain tied to political and economic developments over the last century in a country that has gone from rapid modernization to a sour and short-lived romance with socialism, and on to what seems to have become a lasting union with neoliberalism. Unsurprisingly, as Chile has committed itself, in broad strokes, to capital and consumption (see Han 2012), Palestinian Chileans have found a new sense of freedom in conducting their business and going about their business—of all kinds—the way they see fit.

Meanwhile, to many, the notion of family extends well beyond the intimate domain. As Laila expressed it to me, "Even when we don't get along, it's like . . . it's the blood, ultimately we're all family." In Laila's understanding, the notion of family expands to encompass a forever changing but solidly centered network of Palestinian Chileans in Santiago, some of whom Laila sometimes found herself in conflict with but whom she entertained no idea of cutting herself loose from. Despite certain frustrations, the sense that they were part of an extended family of Palestinian Chileans meant that people like Laila stayed committed to the Palestinian establishment.

Managing Difference

There is a long history of organized and institutionalized Palestinian life in Santiago. The first specifically Palestinian—rather than Arab or Ottoman— organizations and institutions began springing up in the Chilean capital in the early decades of the twentieth century. As was discovered through archival work during my fieldwork, the predecessor of Club Deportivo Palestino, Club Sportivo Palestina, was founded as early as 1916, and in 1917 the first Palestinian Orthodox church—the Catedral Ortodoxa San Jorge—was built in the heart of Patronato. Newspapers oriented toward the Arab world and Palestine in particular, albeit mostly written in Spanish, began surfacing in the 1930s, with the popular *Al Damir* remaining at the forefront since its launch in the wake of the Second Intifada[8] at the turn of the twenty-first century (Baeza 2014a; El-Attar 2011; see also Pacheco 2006).

Since its inauguration, Club Palestino has grown into the hub of Palestinian communal life in Santiago. As an institution, Club Palestino was founded in 1938 and had its first home in downtown Santiago's Santo Domingo Street (Torrejón Vasquez 2011). In 1948, the building on Santo Domingo was put up for sale, and soon after, the club moved to its current location in Las Condes. Without a doubt, the move from central Santiago to the outskirts of the city came in the wake of increased wealth and influence among its constituency. With the move came more land than would ever have been possible to attain downtown, and, at least as important, a place among Santiago's elite in what is now considered one of the most upscale districts of the Chilean capital. Club Palestino is first and foremost a recreational space, and one designed for various forms of socializing. I will return to the club in much more detail in chapter 4, but for now suffice it to note that the layout of the establishment invites a wide array of collective endeavors: with a large gym and swimming pools, tennis courts and football fields, banquet halls and cafés, as well as meeting rooms and lounges—all surrounded and connected by undulating lawns—the club can and does facilitate anything from leisurely strolls to intimate meetings and large gatherings.

It becomes clear at Club Palestino that familial and organized Palestinianness are two sides of the same coin, not least owing to the fact that membership of this and certain other Palestinian institutions hinges on bloodlines and family names. To become a member of the prominent club, one must be able to trace one's descent back to Palestine—something that rarely seems an issue, given the tight-knit relationships that exist between many families, and not least the revealing nature of family names that makes Palestinian Chileans so easily recognized, especially by one another. While certain events at Club Palestino were open to the public during my time in Santiago, unlimited access to the club's facilities and a say in institutional matters depended in most cases on formal membership. First and foremost, the club is a place that fosters and sustains a certain intimacy that characterizes communal Palestinian life as an everyday phenomenon in the Chilean capital. It is where kids can take a swim in the pool, adults can get together for a drink, and friends can play a game of football or indulge in somewhat less athletic games at the bowling alley in the main building. This intimacy, in turn, allows for a certain closing off of the Palestinian establishment, not least when it comes to memory politics and its contentious character as a postdictatorship phenomenon in the Chilean context.

Although leisure activities are a priority at the club, it also offers meeting rooms and banquet halls for more serious endeavors and is home to several Palestinian Chilean organizations. Among these, the Federación Palestina de Chile (the Palestinian Federation of Chile, referred to in what follows as the Federation) is by far the largest and most influential Palestinian organization at the club and in the country. According to its own website, the Federation represents Chile's Palestinian community in a very broad sense of the term and bases this authority on wide-reaching engagement with Chileans of Palestinians descent.[9] Furthermore, it is the only Palestinian diaspora organization in Chile to base its legitimacy on nationwide democratic elections and other ongoing attempts to build bridges between scattered networks of Palestinian Chileans around the country. Its significance shows not only in the respect it receives within Palestinian Chilean circles, however; the Federation is also the go-to organization when reporters and journalists look for comments on the current state of affairs in Palestine, and its leadership regularly publish commentary on their own website, in print dailies, and via other online media. For all intents and purposes, the Federation functions as the loudest voice among Palestinians and their descendants in Chile.

While this institution, with its history, size, and realm of influence, remains an essential gathering point and collective voice for Palestinian Chileans, it is flanked by an increasing number of smaller organizations. One of the most remarkable of these organizations, and one with a decades-old history, is UGEP. Itself the product of both the long history of the Palestinian presence in Chile and a global diasporic engagement with the Palestinian cause, the General Union of Palestinian Students was officially founded in Cairo in 1959, and, as Laurie Brand (1988, 628) writes, it "gradually developed branches throughout the Arab world and beyond and has served as a prime vehicle for the political mobilization of young Palestinians." Indeed, as Sayegh (2013, 25) likewise has pointed out, the organization "was a crucial building block of the post-1948 national movement."

In Santiago, UGEP sprang up in the 1980s around a group of dedicated students, several of whom would continue to be prominent members of the Palestinian establishment as well as part of the broader social and political elite in Santiago. Indeed, the establishment of UGEP in the Chilean capital followed in the wake of heightened efforts by the Palestine Liberation Organization (PLO)[10] to unify and mobilize people of Palestinian descent throughout Latin America (Baeza 2014a).[11] Following the Oslo Peace Accords, however, UGEP was dismantled in the 1990s and was only brought back to life in the wake of the Second Intifada around the year 2000. Since then, various leaderships have managed to reinvent UGEP as one of the most notable Palestinian Chilean organizations, and it lags behind only the Federation in visibility. During my fieldwork, UGEP offered a range of events: film screenings and mini-conferences, public debates and protest marches, as well as informative art installations and other interventions.

The reach of UGEP, however, still seemed limited during my time with the organization. While UGEP is in principle open to anyone, the leadership positions are open only to people of Palestinian descent. If familial ties to Palestine are not evident—and in most, if not all, cases they seem to go unexamined, as those involved have known one another for years—potential candidates are expected to provide proof of their Palestinian lineage by producing legal documents showing the occurrence of a Palestinian surname no further back than two generations. The same rules apply to those who wish to vote in UGEP leadership elections. In reality, while UGEP members have at times lamented the fact that their core group is often in the precarious situation of shrinking over the course of the school year as students' attention drifts toward exams and other obligations, very few people join the ranks of the organization from outside a fairly narrow network of young Palestinian Chileans.[12] During my time in Santiago, the core group of UGEP members counted two young people, besides myself, who had no family ties to Palestine, but who had gradually become more and more engaged via their Palestinian Chilean friends. Our presence apart, however, the organization did not reach far beyond a tight-knit group, and our meetings were almost exclusively held at Club Palestino, with the exception of the few times we met for more informal discussions in the homes of UGEP members. The group's activities limited themselves almost exclusively to well-known cultural and social registers, a tendency that was further solidified by a general reluctance to cooperate with non-Palestinian organizations and institutions—an issue I will return to in more detail later on.[13]

Moreover, the makeup of UGEP, from its leadership to its members and supporters, reflects the impact of one institution above any others: the Colegio Árabe, Santiago's Arab private school. Located in Las Condes, with a beautiful park and one of Santiago's biggest shopping centers as neighbors, Colegio Árabe tends primarily to the children of the Palestinian Chileans who now live in the affluent neighborhoods east of the city center. Following its establishment in

1978, the school operated out of Club Palestino for a number of years but moved to its present location in 1990.[14] The current school building fits the school's clientele. The facilities feature large amounts of material references to the Arab world, from the front office right down along the halls to the classrooms; photos, plaques, and white clocks hang alongside one another at the entrance, each clock showing the current time of a particular Middle Eastern location. The school is in principle open to all children, but those of Palestinian ancestry make up the large majority of students.[15] Here, children receive formal schooling in all the usual subjects, but their education retains a special focus on the Arab world. Before graduation, each class makes a trip to the Middle East, with the itinerary depending on the current circumstances, but always including the area around Bethlehem. This tour is often remembered as a time when students experience an intensified connection both with one another and with the land from which their ancestors came to Chile—something I will return to in chapter 4.

According to Laila, it was not until she was transferred to Colegio Árabe half-way through school that she really got in touch with the communal Palestinian sphere in Santiago. She had always known the Palestinian side of her family well and had even gone to Club Palestino with her family as a child. But apart from her extended family, she had never really connected with other Palestinian Chileans, and since politics were not discussed in her childhood home, she knew very little of what lay behind the continuing Palestinian struggle. At the school, however, she was confronted with previously unknown details of what being Palestinian meant to her Palestinian Chilean peers, and her background came to take on new meaning. Colegio Árabe thus became to Laila what it still is to many young Chileans of Palestinian background: an education in becoming Palestinian in Santiago.

Even children too young to have started school were offered an initiation into shared Palestinianness at Club Palestino during my fieldwork. A series of events under the banner "Yo Soy Palestino" (I Am Palestinian) was a long-standing staple at the club and gathered dozens of kids and their parents for monthly play sessions centered on all things Palestine. The sessions usually featured different activities and storytelling and included a lunch of freshly made shawarma sandwiches and sodas. During my time in Santiago, UGEP leadership was also involved in these events and had agreed to lend out a few of its members to teach a bit of the heavier, political subject matter to the older children. The Yo Soy Palestino events carried great importance as an early schooling into Palestinianness, both to parents and to those who organized activities for the youngest members at the club month after month, even when most of the kids were running around screaming and playing rather than paying careful attention to their lessons.

To Laila, being a student at Colegio Árabe entailed not just learning about her Palestinian background and about how others engaged with Palestine and the Arab world from Santiago. Having had a hard time at her previous schools, for her Colegio Árabe became a kind of refuge, a place where she could finally fit in. During one of our many conversations, she explained, "When I went to school [before moving to Colegio Árabe] I was stared at because I came to class with expensive backpacks, and they called me *cuica* [snob]. . . . I saw a lot of resentment on the part of the Chileans.[16] They just couldn't be happy seeing that someone else was doing well, working harder." Through Laila's comments on her experience of standing out and getting picked on at an ordinary school in Santiago, she positioned herself apart from "the Chileans" (*los chilenos*), all the while reiterating the narrative of Palestinian success as being derived from hard work, a quality that, from Laila's perspective, was not quite appreciated among her previous classmates. Laila's experiences had undoubtedly stayed with her, and her self-concept reflected a troubled relationship with those who did not belong to her circle of Palestinian Chilean family and friends: "The last thing I feel is Chilean. Let's see . . . I don't feel like I share the Chilean culture. I don't feel like I have the same aspirations as the Chileans do, I don't have the same ideas as them." Besides her much-extended family of Palestinian Chilean relatives and peers, Laila concluded, "no one else will ever understand me, and I will never really understand what the Chileans are thinking. . . . I will never understand other ways of thinking because *I wasn't there.*"

The last bit of Laila's commentary on herself and "the Chileans" was especially telling. She had lived all her life in the Chilean capital, and although much of her time had been spent among those who share her Palestinian heritage, Laila's language was full of Chilean slang, her accent was unmistakably Chilean, her clothes had come out of the malls in Las Condes and the small shops in Patronato, even her ideas and aspirations had undeniably been formed within the Chilean context. At the same time, her statement spoke volumes about how Laila perceived her own position vis-à-vis her fellow Chileans and pointed to a much broader tendency within the Palestinian establishment, namely to maintain a certain shared distance to what surrounds it. This distance, in turn, had much to do with the overarching emphasis on the familiar that continues to color so much of Palestinian life in Santiago. During another of my chats with Laila, she returned to the theme of family. Referring back to her own experiences of standing out among Chileans, she asserted that "that's what people don't see. People see that we have money, but they don't see that we're all one big family." For that same reason, she went on to explain, there will always be a sense of separateness between the Palestinian establishment and the Chile beyond it; "I think this all makes it difficult for people to mix with each other. When we're so different . . . I think it's possible to mix, but never completely. We might have a demonstration with both Palestinians and Chileans, but afterward the Palestinians will go their way and the Chileans will go theirs." Indeed, she said, "it's always like that. The Palestinians [*los palestinos*] stay together and don't mix with Chileans. We're together but not jumbled up [*estamos juntos pero no revueltos*]."

Beyond the Familiar

While the reality of Palestinian social life in Chile is, of course, more nuanced than in Laila's portrayal, her observations did seem to strike a chord with her peers, at least to an extent. Although many Chileans of Palestinian descent went about their everyday lives as Chileans, with little or no contact with the communal Palestinian sphere, many others seemed to have tied themselves so closely to their common ground that they had become almost stuck in it. In daily life, the infrastructure of the Palestinian establishment in Santiago means that a particular distance to the broader Chilean social and political environment is easily maintained. As described above, Las Condes is home to Club Palestino, the Palestinian Embassy, and Colegio Árabe. Moreover, the district is home to a large portion of the Palestinian Chilean families that currently reside in the capital, along with several family-owned businesses, restaurants, and shops. The relative proximity of these Palestinian domains interplays with the exclusive nature of each of them—public business venues aside—to make for something of a distinct Palestinian nook in the urban landscape.[17]

More than once, Laila and I got to talking about Club Palestino. Like many of her friends, Laila recognized how closed-off the club seemed, and she had sometimes expressed frustration at how secluded it was—lamenting especially the limited reach of the many events and campaigns that continued to speak to the same audience again and again. In her view, however, there was a good reason for this to be the case. To Laila, the separation from wider society that marked both the location of Club Palestino and the life within it was, at least in part, a consequence of the animosity felt by the first Palestinian immigrants. In her words, "They [Chileans] discriminated so much against the Palestinians that came to this country that they learned to discriminate themselves. My grandfather had an Ottoman passport, and he was always 'el turco.'" Going back to her grandfather and his hard work as her starting point, Laila continued to give her take on what had happened: "The Palestinians are hard workers and put in a lot of effort, so when they came here, they worked a lot. When the Chileans saw that the Palestinians were making lots of money while they themselves, who had been here for such a long time, had not made a single *peso*, they said

'Ah, we don't want the Arabs.'"[18] While the foundation for separation may have been laid by discrimination, however, those tied to the Palestinian establishment had done their bit in severing their community from its surroundings. Even to Laila, as she elaborated, "the fault isn't completely with the Chileans— the Palestinians went and closed themselves off in their own bubble." In Laila's take on the matter, secluding themselves in Club Palestino and elsewhere had been a counterreaction to discrimination, albeit one that was perhaps a bit too severe.

In the 1980s, around the time of the First Intifada[19] and in the midst of dictatorship, political currents were strong in both Palestine and Chile. At the same time, for Palestinian Chileans who were critical of dictatorship, engaging with the Palestinian cause became a subtler and less dangerous way of expressing opposition to Pinochet's junta than engaging directly in protest against military rule. For others, however, a focus on Palestine legitimized a lack of engagement with Chilean politics. Subsequently, the early 1990s saw Pinochet give up the presidential seat, and the Oslo Accords quieted things down in Palestine and Israel, however transiently. Around that time, political engagement seemed to reach a low point within Santiago's Palestinian establishment. As previously noted, UGEP dissolved as a direct response to the peace process. According to Alex, one of the people who helped reboot the organization in the early 2000s, those involved in UGEP at the time simply thought the "job done" and saw no reason to continue its work. Around the time of the Second Intifada, however, an active political engagement with Palestine was reawakened. UGEP came back to life under the auspices of a new leadership of young students, and in early 2002 thousands of people manifested their concern for Palestine through a demonstration that culminated in front of the presidential palace at La Moneda (see Baeza 2005; El-Attar 2011).

During the time of my fieldwork, political engagement with Palestine was front and center at the vast majority of activities within the Palestinian establishment in Santiago, either explicitly or implicitly. Meanwhile, several decades into the era of postdictatorship, the consequences of the political developments in Chile since the early 1970s were, at best, subtly expressed. Although migration to Chile had begun before any real attempts at implementation of the Zionist vision in Palestine, the Palestinian establishment in Santiago was in many ways born out of catastrophe, particularly *the* catastrophe for Palestinians, namely the *Nakba* of 1948 (see Peteet 2005, 3). The multifaceted violence that has been playing out in Palestine and Israel ever since has had, and continues to have, a profound effect on social, cultural, and political life for those associated with the Palestinian establishment in the Chilean capital. It frames the struggle that they, regardless of political affiliation, return to time and again.[20]

While the situation in Palestine informs much of daily life within Palestinian Chilean circles in Santiago, it is not the only political issue that has some influence on the texture of the quotidian. Rather, a much more understated instance of strife pertains to exactly that Chilean reality, past and present, that the Palestinian establishment seems to have become somewhat removed from. That larger Chilean dynamic has a long and intricate past, not least among Santiago's Palestinian Chileans, and is a subject that I will delve into with much more detail in the following chapters. To set the stage for the considerations to follow, however, it should be noted that to understand the ins and outs of the Palestinian Chilean commitment to Palestine, that commitment must be scrutinized in relation to a deep-reaching Chilean disunity that harks back to societal ruptures taking place in the time leading up to the military coup almost five decades ago. As pointed out earlier, many Palestinian Chilean businesspeople had much to gain from Pinochet's neoliberal agenda and continue to profit from the political reality of the Chile that has developed since then. For that reason and others, many still support *la derecha*. At the same time, many others were against Pinochet's rule and have gone as far as connecting being anti-Pinochet with being pro-Palestine. Categorizing politics within this sort of overarching logic is not uncommon, and for those who see the similarities between the repressive nature of the Chilean dictatorship of the past and of the Israeli advances in Palestine today, the fact that so many of their peers think differently can be difficult to understand and accept.

One young woman who considered herself left wing, on matters both Chilean and Palestinian, was Ana. She was a familiar presence at Club Palestino and almost always showed up when there was a demonstration or other political event centered on Palestine. Ana's position within the sphere of the Palestinian establishment was somewhat ambiguous, however, though it was clear that she was not always comfortable with the way things were. When I asked her about it on a chilly afternoon when we were alone, sitting at a café downtown, she said, "I don't understand it very well, but the Arab community in Chile . . . the majority is right wing. It's very weird." To Ana, this fact simply did not make sense. "I don't understand how someone can be right wing and support the Palestinian cause at the same time . . . because Israel represents, in the Middle East, a colonial power that uses repressive mechanisms. But here in Chile, it's like 'we're super Palestinian, but we're right wing. Just go ahead and kill the Mapuche!'"[21]

Hinting at a certain commonality between the Palestinian cause and the struggle of Chile's indigenous Mapuche population against state violence, land confiscations, and ultimately dispossession, Ana painted a dramatic picture of indifference among some Palestinian Chileans. Surely, no one had actually suggested to "go ahead and kill the Mapuche," but Ana certainly pointed to an almost conspicuous lack of involvement with non-Palestinian issues on the part of the

Palestinian establishment. Indeed, no ties were forged, and no collective solidarity was expressed with the Mapuche cause—or any other political struggle, for that matter—during my time in Santiago.[22] That this was the case, I argue, had much to do with the complex dynamics of memory and forgetting between post-dictatorship Chile and occupied Palestine.

To Ana, right-wing politics and the Palestinian cause were absolutely incompatible, but combining the two was nevertheless a prevalent practice within the Palestinian establishment. Unlike Ana, Laila considered herself conservative and was very vocal about this fact with me. Around the time of the presidential elections in late 2013, we had many a talk about what the future might look like under a new head of state. I had quickly come to realize that Laila, like the rest of her family, supported the conservative candidate Evelyn Matthei, but she only fully elaborated after it had become clear, following a second round of voting, that socialist Michelle Bachelet would be reinstated as president of Chile. During a lunch of stuffed vine leaves and tabbouleh in Patronato, Laila confirmed that she and the rest of her family had all voted for Matthei and were sorely disappointed with the outcome of the elections. The reinstatement of Bachelet seemed a veritable disaster to Laila, and as we continued our conversation, it became clear that Laila's politics had much to do with her particular background. In an irritated tone, she suggested that the prospect of increased welfare programs was the reason why people voted for Bachelet: to get bonuses. Distancing herself from her objects of analysis, Laila explained that "we know we have to work if we want to eat," referring to her family and the wider Palestinian establishment and suggesting that this sets them apart from most ordinary Chileans. Soon after, Laila went on to conclude that "we were better off with Pinochet"—that "nothing excuses the murders," but that he did a lot to help businesspeople and immigrants. According to her, ousted president Allende wanted good things only for "Chileans, not immigrants."[23] In contrast, Laila explained, Pinochet treated Chilean and non-Chilean alike and supported all entrepreneurs. For that, he was better for the country and for Palestinian Chilean businesses, and since Matthei supported Pinochet and his line, Laila supported Matthei.

The openness to immigrants and their descendants that Laila perceived to be present in Pinochet's approach and to which she attached particular importance did not seem to easily translate into an openness to the experiences of those whose lives might have improved under Allende had his term in La Moneda not been cut short. The somewhat paradoxical logics at play here speak to wider issues of how political projects simultaneously rely on localized mnemonic boundaries and connections forged across distance. Ana and Laila clearly approached politics from far different angles. While Ana highlighted solidarity against repressive regimes, Laila focused on the interests of herself, her family, and her immediate surroundings. These disparate perspectives made for an odd tension within the Palestinian Chilean sphere—an always underlying unease that is illuminating of memory as a political force in complex contexts where the present and the absent are negotiable phenomena.

In this chapter, I have sought to outline some of the social and historical factors that constitute the contemporary Palestinian presence in Santiago. Through powerful narratives of adversity—both in the old land and for Chile's first Palestinian immigrants and their descendants—a long-held idea of Palestinians as people that prevail by way of hard work seems to have become entrenched. Meanwhile, a shared commitment to Palestine and to keeping Palestine present, as it were, binds people like Ana and Laila together toward a common goal that surpasses ideological differences and that hinges on a complex politics of memory with implications far beyond notions of hard work and success. In the following chapter I explore this politics and the mnemonic tensions it carries with it and suggest that the sort of memory at play here is ultimately moving, characterized by continuous motion across and beyond temporal and spatial boundaries while harboring affective qualities.

STAGING THE PAST

Many of the people I met throughout fieldwork gave clear accounts of their fami-lies' composition and movement over time, both in Chile and back in Palestine, often referring to meticulously produced family trees and recalling the memories of past generations. At the same time, broader narratives of exodus, violence, and dispossession were collectively shared and often reiterated during informal conversations as well as during formal commemorative ceremonies and public events. In May 2014 in Santiago, a range of such events was planned during a week entirely dedicated to commemorating the Nakba. It was a week filled with various smaller events, some overlapping, but all leading to a grand finale of music and dance designated a "festival of solidarity" (*festival de solidaridad*) by the main organizer, the Federación Palestina de Chile.

One of the first events of the week, held on Monday evening, featured the Pal-estinian ambassador to Chile reflecting on "sixty-six years of the Nakba, memo-ries of a continuing catastrophe" (*66 años del Nakba, recuerdos de una catástrofe que continúa*)—a formulation that likewise served as the event's subheading in the promotional materials. The ambassador's talk certainly set the tone for the week to come. It was a week dedicated to commemorating the past, but the scope of its events went well beyond the already passed. Rather, as the formulation above intimates, the lectures, debates, and performances of this week looked to the present and the future as much as they looked to the past. Indeed, those who participated in organizing and carrying out this weeklong commemoration rec-ognized that these categories of time and experience should be approached all together rather than fixed into separate domains. Without a doubt, the event that featured the Palestinian ambassador sought to look back upon the more than six decades that had already passed since the commencement of the Nakba and the coinciding establishment of the state of Israel. At the same time, its organizers and audience displayed an astute awareness of the continuation of this catastrophe through the present and into the future. In the mere act of naming this event, the people behind it had tapped directly into the complexity of memory, experience, and the passing of time.

Just as remembrance and commemoration do not limit their scope to the past, so do they not play out in a political vacuum. Remembering the Nakba in Santiago involves calling attention to the still unsolved problem of Palestinian dispossession and the continuing Israeli encroachment on Palestinian spaces and lives. At the same time, this memory work unavoidably takes place within a local and national context still grappling with the aftereffects of another unsettling and prolonged event, namely that of Chilean dictatorship. In this chapter, I take my cue from the events of that week of Nakba commemorations and use them as an offset to explore the dynamics of moving memory—a phenomenon that refers to overlapping pasts, presents, and futures all at once—as it is confronted with local political circumstances that render it impossible to confine and difficult to steer in any singular direction.

In Santiago de Chile, engaging in the collective and highly politicized work of diasporic Palestinian remembrance entails navigating a wider political reality that ties in the recent history of Israeli settler colonialism with a Chilean history of political violence, most notably against indigenous populations and other dissidents. Both histories are unconfinable to particular nation-states and are rather wrapped up in global flows and power dynamics that, in both cases, have relied heavily on US influence and are indelibly tied to centuries of wide-reaching imperialist projects, from those of Spanish colonization and Ottoman rule to Nazi Germany. The historical developments that have become foundational to present-day Chile, Palestine, and Israel unsurprisingly continue to have great bearing on contestations over what the past, present, and future might entail for Palestinian Chileans and many others with ties to either of those lands and what they represent. Rather than treat the issue of Palestinian Chilean memory politics in isolation, then, I treat it as an ethnographic case study in the intricacies of how remembrance—as a future-oriented practice as much as an engagement with the already passed—is negotiated within and beyond porous geographical and sociopolitical boundaries.

In this chapter I aim, on the one hand, to carve out the minutiae and vicissitudes of Palestinian Chilean remembrance and its inherent tensions as they play out within Chilean and Palestinian realms of memory politics. Both these contexts remain marked by troubled and continuously troubling pasts, as well as efforts at reckoning that have followed prolonged periods of instability and conflict. On the other hand, I open an investigation into the affective aspects of moving memory by considering how remembrance *moves* people to take political action—or refrain from doing so.

Reflecting tensions in how memory is both *felt* and *practiced*, I argue, a wavering between remembrance and oblivion has come to characterize much of Palestinian Chilean social life within the mnemonic field of tension between the Chilean and the Palestinian—a field of tension that is subject to constant flows of stories and people through always permeable geographical and sociopolitical boundaries and that thus itself remains in flux. As will be explored further in what follows, both Palestine and Chile have seen decades of tumultuous encounters with and over the politics of memory, not least through various forms of memory activism centered on grassroots efforts to uncover past instances of violence and to remember victims, events, and places that might have otherwise been lost with time (see Anderman 2015; see also French 2012). In both Chile and Palestine, memory has taken on notable political significance, and a reckoning with the past continues to be a reckoning with past politics and the consequences of past political actions. Put quite simply, then, the sort of memory at stake here is by no means separate from the relations, particular histories, and especially the politics that permeate both narratives told and the context within which the past is managed (see Gillis 1994). This particular point will continue to assert its relevance throughout this book. Besides foregrounding the entanglements between politics and memory, I begin here to open an investigation into how memory comes to move in and across space as well as time. To unfold the analysis of this dynamic, the present chapter will also serve as a more general introduction to the histories of political conflict that interweave in the fabric of Palestinian life in Santiago.

Remembering the Nakba in Recoleta

The grand finale to the week of Nakba commemorations was a widely publicized outdoor concert dubbed "Chile sings for Palestine" (*Chile canta a Palestina*). The event was held in the open courtyard of Recoleta town hall, just north of the city center, where plastic chairs had been set up in extension of the concrete stairs leading down into the small square below, empty apart from the tall stage and light fixtures that had been installed in preparation for the evening. Alongside Palestinian Chilean dance troupes and speakers, the program featured performances by folk veterans Illapu and the popular rapper Ana Tijoux. When I arrived at this makeshift amphitheater the place was already full, with flags and banners swaying against the backdrop of the dark autumn sky above the brimming bleachers and seats. On either side of the imposing stage, large white-and-red banners had been suspended from the scaffolding that framed it, each reading "Vivir mejor es posible"—Living better is possible. I found Andrea sitting at the very front, surrounded by friends and acquaintances from the Federation, UGEP, and from the wider social circles centered on Club Palestino. Like most of them, she had traveled from the city's northeast to a district she only rarely visited.

In many ways, Recoleta did not seem the most obvious place to set the stage for a Palestinian solidarity event, especially given the fact that the majority of Palestinian Chilean institutions, organizations, and families are based elsewhere. Of course, the Patronato neighborhood is technically part of the Recoleta municipality. However, that the town hall of this Santiago district should be chosen as the location for several of the events of the Nakba commemoration week had a more straightforward explanation than the relative proximity of Patronato. Since 2012, Palestinian Chilean sociologist, writer, architect, and public intellectual Daniel Jadue of the Communist Party had been mayor of this particular Santiago borough while at the same time tending to a position as spokesperson and vice president of the Federation. Indeed, Mayor Jadue was among the few speakers of the night and agitatedly called for solidarity and celebrating diversity when he took the stage, welcoming the people of Recoleta and his Palestinian Chilean network to join together in showing support for Palestine.

Another prominent speaker was Mauricio Abu-Ghosh, the president of the Federation and a widely known spokesperson for what he usually referred to simply as Chile's Palestinian community (*la comunidad palestina de Chile*). His short speech acted as a sort of intermission between musical performances and followed a show of *dabke* routines—part of the Palestinian folklore that the audience had been promised in the flyers that had been circulated beforehand.[1] As soon as Abu-Ghosh had come onstage and grabbed the microphone, he got straight to the point. "I would like to start by asking a question," he said, his voice loud and clear through the large speakers. "What would you do if in the middle of the night armed strangers came into your house, shooting, killing your parents, throwing you into exile, and negating the existence of your people? You would resist, right? You would resist!" Thus drawing threads between the Palestinian experience and the experiences of those forcibly removed from their homes in the Chilean context—from displaced indigenous communities to the victims of the junta—Abu-Ghosh briefly paused. A few people in the crowd answered with indistinct shouting, one or two people were heard clapping, but the sounds died out quickly as Abu-Ghosh continued:

> The Palestinian people have been resisting for sixty-six years, resisting the biggest massacre that has taken place in modern history. Zionism occupied Palestine and took the majority of Palestinian land: the land that has borne fruit, and that has borne fruit that you continue to see, for instance in the mayor Jadue, for instance in these young people that you just saw dancing the *dabke*. That *dabke*, to be sure, is part of Palestinian culture. Palestinian culture manifests itself in many forms. The *dabke*, which is of this culture, is resistance. It is showing the world that the Palestinian people are alive and will stay alive. Years have passed, and the Palestinian people have continued to resist. And that is a commitment that not only we make, but that you are making with your presence here tonight.

As the crowd cheered, with more conviction this time around, Abu-Ghosh looked out to the rows of people in front of him, and then carried on:

> A diligent Zionist once said that the old will die and the young will forget. The old probably died, but the young did not forget. The young are here, and they are here because they are resisting. The home of the Palestinian people is in resistance. They have been resisting for sixty-six years and will continue to resist until they have a free and dignified state, where Christians, Jews, and Muslims can live together, a state for all. Thank you all. ¡Viva Chile! ¡Viva Palestina![2]

The people around me applauded and whistled loudly, and Andrea held her phone up to capture the moment on camera. I had already heard Abu-Ghosh speak many times and knew his style of emotionally laden rhetoric and fiery delivery. On the occasion of commemorating the Nakba, it was no surprise that he should focus on the topic of Palestinian resistance and tie the concept to the very presence of *dabke* dancers in Recoleta on this dark evening during the cool Chilean fall. Indeed, the idea that acts of remembrance such as this Nakba commemoration could be nothing less than acts of resistance was widely repeated within Palestinian Chilean organizations such as the Federation and UGEP. In his brief oration, Abu-Ghosh succinctly expressed not only a collective concern with the Palestinian struggle, but indeed with remembrance as a crucial part of that struggle. At the grand finale to the Nakba commemoration week, the connection between remembrance and resistance became all the clearer. At the heart of Abu-Ghosh's speech on this particular evening, as well as many others, was a particular narrative of a particular form of resistance—a resistance thick with the past and thick with memory.

In many ways, while the focus on the stage was unequivocally on Palestine, the event at Recoleta town hall displayed a certain convergence between remembering the Palestinian Nakba and remembering repression and dissent closer to home. Taking place within the wider landscape of Recoleta—both a culturally diverse and relatively underprivileged neighborhood (Álvarez 2011; Márquez 2014)—the mix of Palestinian dance performances and the spectacle delivered by musicians whose work is deeply embedded in the Chilean political context seemed to reflect an overlapping of worlds likewise evident in the very influx of Palestinian Chileans to this part of the city on the night of the show. Illapu continue to represent the Chilean *nueva canción* tradition and have been dealing with sociopolitical issues in their music over the course of a career spanning decades, including a period of exile during the dictatorship. Ana Tijoux, meanwhile, was born to Chilean parents in exile and has made a mark on the scene as a politically conscious artist since returning to Chile, not least with the track "Somos Sur"—We Are the South—a 2014 collaboration with Palestinian-British artist Shadia Mansour. Just weeks before the Nakba show, Tijoux had received abuse by audience members during a festival performance, when shouts of "cara de nana" were hurled at the stage, insinuating that Tijoux resembled the domestic workers, often of Mapuche descent, who continue to be a prevalent feature of upper-middle-class life in Santiago and who are most often referred to precisely as *nanas*. In response to those who sought to insult her, she expressed pride at the comparison and tweeted, "I am that *nana* face, that face that resembles yours."[3] As an artist and public figure, Tijoux continues to tap into the intersectional nature of social injustice in the Chilean context, and her presence on the stage on that evening in Recoleta placed class politics and the Mapuche struggle amid calls for the liberation of Palestine.

The musical presence of Illapu and Ana Tijoux was not the only marker of the connection between this event and wider antiauthoritarian and decolonial struggles, however. Concentrated behind the small group of specially invited guests—politicians and community leaders who had been seated at the front—or standing around to the side, drifting from the backstage area inside the building to our right, many familiar faces from Club Palestino and beyond were watching the show, chatting away, and waving at each other across the rows of chairs set up for the event. Farther behind them, however, unfamiliar faces characterized the large crowd. Although a few Palestinian flags hovered above the audience, most of the bits of fabric that swayed in the soft breeze of the evening carried the colors of the Mapuche flag. It was clear that the Palestinian Chilean VIPs, dancers, and audience members had moved out of Club Palestino and the rest of the

Northeast of the city and into a political territory where the Palestinian struggle was not the only one that mattered, and where commemorating the Nakba also involved commemorating the lived reality of Chile's indigenous population.

The Mapuche are but one of the indigenous groups who trace their origins to areas within current-day Chile. Even so, the Mapuche and their struggle over rights to land and liberty have taken on an almost mythical aura ever since they became one of the first indigenous peoples in the Americas to fight off the Spanish conquistadors (see Crow 2013, 10; see also Collier and Sater 2004, 4–5). Mapuche resistance has become a prime example of popular struggle, even heroism, in the face of oppression, and as part of this struggle, memory plays an important role. Macarena Gómez-Barris (2015, 78) has argued that for the Mapuche of present-day Chile, memory has become "an activator of forms of expressive resistance." To be sure, this could be said of many similar cases, and indeed the politicization of remembrance has come to bear on myriad peoples and places across the globe. Likewise, Gómez-Barris's contention might easily be expanded to consider memory and the political as mutually mobilizing. While memory often acts as activator, spurring people into action as they are moved by the recurring presence of past and present injustice, the opposite is just as often the case. Indeed, as already pointed out, memory is continuously invoked and activated as part of Palestinian counteraction to both subtle and more overtly aggressive forms of Israeli violence.

To some, the Palestinian and the Mapuche struggles are two sides of a worldwide imperialist coin. As Andrea, who vehemently supports the Mapuche in their quest for self-determination, said to me over lunch one day, "The Mapuche struggle is a left-wing struggle, as is the Palestinian." While this commonality might have placed the Mapuche presence neatly alongside the Palestinian at the commemoration event at Recoleta's town hall, the relationship between what Gómez-Barris (2015) calls "Mapuche mnemonics" and the wider context of memory politics in Chile adds a layer of complexity to the matter. As Joanna Crow (2013) has pointed out, the collective reckoning that followed in the wake of dictatorship left little room for Mapuche memories and a much further-reaching history of struggle in the Mapuche heartland of Auracanía to the south of the capital city. This, as I will return to in chapter 3, reflects a lack of inclusion that extends far into the Palestinian establishment in Santiago and that by and large hinges on the awkward tension between insistently rose-colored images of the Pinochet legacy, on the one hand, and more critical perspectives on remembrance on the other.

In that context, the Mapuche struggle has become more than a struggle for territory and sovereignty over that territory. Especially in the decades following the 1973 coup, it has become about securing presence and visibility in a context where the preoccupation has been with memory work of a different kind and with reference to an instance of state oppression that is limited in its temporal, spatial, and political scope to dealing with particular facets of the dictatorship era. The flags blazoning the emblem of the Mapuche over the crowd that had gathered to commemorate the Nakba signaled solidarity between two causes to which memory and presence are central, but they also secured that distinct Mapuche visibility on an evening where their cause might have otherwise remained unseen and unmentioned. Against the inescapable message of "living better is possible" that hung suspended at either side of the stage throughout the evening, imaginings of a brighter future served as the literal as well as figurative backdrop to the proceedings. A central question remained unanswered, however: For whom is living better possible?

Watershed Moments: 1948 and 1973

I opened up this chapter with a recapitulation of the main event of the Nakba commemoration week because as a particular moment, it contained so much of the stuff of memory that forms part of everyday life in Santiago. While remembrance often presents itself in much more subtle, everyday forms—not least among Palestinian Chileans who have made the memory of Palestine part of a diasporic political project—the commemoration that was performed in various ways during the Nakba week indeed encapsulated not only the perceived power and potential in remembering collectively, but also some of the most pressing tensions that exist within the realm of memory in this context.

As I sought to show above, this simultaneously commemorative and celebratory festival displayed unequivocally the unconfinability of memory in the Chilean context. At one level, memory experienced and performed as a social phenomenon seems to be always entangled in political struggles of one kind or another. At another level, these struggles seem to always be on the verge of—or actually—spilling over into one another, leaving it virtually impossible to maintain a guarded perimeter around any one particular mnemo-political project, however it might be staged. While this might potentially entail solidarity across struggles for land, sovereignty, justice, and equality in Chile and beyond—as those who welcomed Palestinian memory into the heartland of Recoleta and Mapuche sympathizers into the heart of a commemoration of the Nakba recognized—it also causes strain as uncomfortable differences come to the fore and memory struggles become struggles over which cause receives the most attention and support. As I will come back to later, Mapuche-Palestinian solidarity retains two elements that are always in tension: the potential in joining forces, and the risk in competing over attention.[4] At either extreme, the wider historical context of postdictatorship Chile can never be put out of play. Both Mapuche resistance and Palestinian memory politics are grounded in a place where 1973 continues to constitute a watershed moment whence all the stuff of the present has followed. As Patricio Guzmán (2010) notes in his film *Nostalgia for the Light*, memory has a gravitational force, and in Chile, this force tends to pull toward those fateful hours on September 11, 1973, and the years that followed the violent power shift of that day.

The trajectory of changing attitudes and engagements with the past in Chilean society, especially since the end of dictatorship in 1990, tells an interesting story of the dynamic relationship between remembrance and oblivion as well as between state actors and the grassroots of memory politics. When, only a few years into the presidency of Allende, Chile experienced a violent coup led by then-general Pinochet, the ideological direction of establishment Chilean politics went topsy-turvy as the Allende administration's socialist vision was cast aside. In the years that followed, the military regime persecuted those who were believed to oppose and pose a threat to its rule while it imposed an ardent neoliberal agenda on all areas of national policy.[5] The years of dictatorship and the political developments that culminated in the military takeover in 1973 have been dealt with in great detail by others (e.g., Collier and Sater 2004; Huneeus 2007; Moulian 1997; Paley 2001; Stern 2006) and are not the main focus here. However, their significance on the present is difficult to overestimate. While many Chileans went into exile abroad, executions, torture, and disappearances were commonplace and made dictatorship-era Chile an infamous case of state violence.[6] This violence, beginning on the day of the coup itself, when Allende was one of the first people to fall victim to his own overthrow, continued on in places that were specially adapted to function as detention centers and torture sites.[7] Some of these, like Villa Grimaldi in Santiago, were later uncovered and remade into physical testaments to what took place within them.[8] Both in the physical and the sociopolitical landscape, then, the dictatorship era remains a mnemonic focal point, and the extent of the crimes committed during that time are still being uncovered to this day.

At the same time, violence is but one side of the story. The other, often repeated by conservative segments of the population and many of the Palestinian Chileans I came to know in Santiago, tells of remarkable economic growth under the junta and the so-called "Chicago Boys" affiliated with it, as well as during the postdictatorship years when their policies have largely been upheld.[9] The ideas that lay behind Pinochet's economic agenda were, to a great extent, based on the free-market dreams of US economists. The foundation for the exchange between Chile and the United States was laid as early as 1955 when a partnership was established between the University of Chicago and Santiago's Universidad

Católica,[10] providing training under Milton Friedman for a large group of Chilean students, some of whom later came to be known precisely as the Chicago Boys (see Alexander 2009, 4; Brender 2010; Paley 2001, 8). While the background for this exchange and the developments that led to it are still contested points, the results of Pinochet's coalition with Chicago-educated economists are clear: growth on the one hand and massive inequality on the other (see Han 2012; Huneeus 2007).[11]

The formal reckoning with the events, and indeed everyday experiences of the Chilean people during dictatorship, would of course only come after Pinochet's stepping down. Especially in the years following the inauguration of Patricio Aylwin, who became the first democratically elected president since the coup, the labor of memory took a hold on the Chilean public and consolidated 1973 as the moment that would always be looked back on as a reference point—indeed a starting point for subsequent developments (see Stern 2010, 122). As with the birth of the Israeli state in 1948, the Chilean coup of 1973 divided the history of a nation into a before and an after, and came to spark a long-lasting preoccupation with memory, albeit with some delay. As Gómez-Barris (2009, 15) writes, "Allende's political action had made visible the social fractures that existed in the nation," but, it might be added, these fractures were only enhanced by the violence that followed Pinochet's takeover and continue to inform and affect what current-day Chileans remember from those years and how they remember (see also Angell 2007).

The year 1973 does not stand alone as a remembered turning point within the context of the Palestinian establishment in Santiago. As the week of Nakba commemorations described above made evident, the establishment of Israel in 1948 constitutes another watershed moment, and one whose presence is notable in the Palestinian sphere at Club Palestino and elsewhere (see Peteet 2005, 3, 20). The military dictatorship also had immense effects on Palestinian Chilean individuals, families, and institutions and in many ways set the tone for the sorts of Palestinianness that could and would be practiced and expressed during the years of Pinochet's rule. The abrupt shift from living under Allende's societal reordering project to taking on a new daily life under the neoliberal reality of Pinochet's Chile was starkly felt across the board, but as in Chilean society more broadly, dictatorship had different consequences for different people; and, as I will return to in more detail, this particular period of a common past is still very much a source of potential disruption.

In contrast, the Nakba has come to attain the status of unifier, smoothing over disparities as it foregrounds agreement on a common cause, namely the Palestinian. As the week of Nakba commemorative events suggested, the establishment of the state of Israel in 1948 has come to be an eternal point of reference within the Palestinian struggle for statehood and self-determination (see, e.g., Conner-ton 2009, 7; Hammer 2005, 43; Peteet 2005; Sa'di and Abu-Lughod 2007). Its centrality holds sway not only within the Palestinian establishment in Santiago and among Chile's Palestinian Chileans. Rather, the Nakba is a point of reference for Palestinians the world over, who often hinge much of their personal and col-lective history on this one event. The Nakba—a word that translates literally as "catastrophe"—was indeed that for the Palestinian people, and its importance does not seem to diminish with time, nor does its very real effects on life in Palestine and beyond. As a traumatic event, as well as a starting point for a past that is still very much part of the present, the Nakba has indeed become "a key event in the Palestinian calendar—the baseline for personal histories and the sorting of generations" (Abu-Lughod and Sa'di 2007, 5, 7). For Palestinian Chil-eans, this watershed moment thus plays multiple roles in experiences of both quotidian Palestinian diasporicity and commemorative events out of the ordi-nary. Indeed, to the people I know in Santiago, Palestinian narratives of the past have come to form a counter-history to common Israeli versions of that same past (see Abu-Lughod and Sa'di 2007). Put differently, Palestinian memory has become countermemory and Palestinian narratives counter-narratives to "the thundering story of Zionism" (Abu-Lughod and Sa'di 2007, 6; see Foucault 1977; Olick and Robbins 1998).[12] In this countermovement of memories, stories, and narratives, staged in opposition to Zionist ideas of the promised land, the Nakba is an eternal point of return.

Of course, the story of 1948, like so many others, has two sides. The Nakba was a catastrophe for Palestinians, but a triumph for the Jews of Palestine who could now call themselves Israeli—not to mention Jews from around the world who could now legally settle in the young state after the so-called Law of Return was implemented in 1950 (see Hass 2011). In the words of Peteet (2008, 15), "If the events of 1948 are narrated by Palestinians as a veritable catastrophe, a moment of radical rupture and a trope for ongoing suffering, for Israelis 1948 serves as a temporal marker of a long-desired restoration and renewal" (see also Assmann 2018). While they also serve as reminders of the parallels between Jewish and Pal-estinian experiences of persecution and erasure, it is precisely these diametrically opposed stories of joy and disaster, of nation born and of nation torn apart, that lend the counter- to Palestinian memory. As long as there are conflicting ideas of what has been and what should be, there will be protest in remembering things differently and in telling a different story of Palestine before and after Israel.

Palestinian Chilean memory in Santiago is in many ways located between the watershed moments of 1948 and 1973. However, these are mere reference points and temporal nodes within much more complex trajectories. The political antag-onism surrounding the events of 1973 in Chile has by and large continued into the twenty-first century and cannot be severed from the far-reaching political currents that allowed the junta to gain power and restructure much of Chilean society with the help of the CIA and the Friedman-trained Chicago Boys (Barder 2013; Kornbluh [2003] 2013); all the while the Nakba and its effects continue to play out within what is more and more commonly referred to as conditions of de facto apartheid (see White 2018). Meanwhile, the immediate aftermath of the Chilean coup on September 11 coincided with the Yom Kippur War of October 1973: a major event in the Middle East as well as a significant moment in broader Cold War politics. In both historical and present terms, then, the Chilean state of (post)dictatorship and the Palestinian Nakba overlap, not only in mundane, localized ways, but also as spatiotemporal nodes in global power dynamics.

Moved by Memory

Among the crowds at the week's events was a young man with an outlook very different from that of Andrea: Tarek. Always with a certain shyness about him and less dominant than several of his peers, Tarek had nonetheless become a key figure in UGEP after earlier political ventures at Colegio Árabe and within smaller and often short-lived Palestinian Chilean youth associations. Among his fellow UGEPers he was well liked, both for putting in an immense effort and for being a friend, never hesitating to offer rides in his car or share his snacks in the restaurant at Club Palestino. During the week of Nakba commemorations Tarek had mainly been working behind the scenes or performing with the team of young *dabke* dancers who so often spent their evenings and weekends either practicing or performing their traditional routines. After the week of commemorations, Tarek's work did not seem to dwindle. A student of law like several of his contemporaries at UGEP, Tarek was equally committed to his extracurricular duties and his studies but often found himself tired and stressed by the magnitude of tasks continuously placed in front of him. As we strolled along the streets of Providencia one afternoon in late autumn, he expressed his disappointment that no one else seemed to take on the level of responsibility that he would like to see within the realm of student mobilization for Palestine, leaving him exhausted with having to perform a leadership role that he did not always seem comfortable with.

Stopping for a cup of coffee before Tarek was off to yet another meeting nearby, we talked about the importance of remembering Palestine and of gathering a wide range of people to commemorate the Nakba as a means of calling attention to the continuation of dispossession and violence even decades after the establishment of the Israeli state. Having grown up "feeling more Palestinian than Chilean" despite his great-grandparents having arrived in Chile over a century ago, Tarek had already traveled to Palestine and had his heart set on spending more time in a place that he described as feeling like home, although he could not quite put his finger on where that feeling came from. When I asked him what it was that made it so important for him to nurture the connection with Palestine—a connection he explained had really been forged upon his entry into the Colegio Árabe, despite a lack of interest among his family for matters regarding the old land—his response was prompt: "I'm working against the prophecy of Golda Meir or Ben-Gurion, or whoever said it, that the young will forget. No, I want to show that that's not the case, we won't forget. Despite the fact that my family didn't flee Israel, I feel the moral responsibility to fight that injustice [perpetrated] against my Palestinian brothers and sisters."

For Tarek, the commitment to Palestine was always at the front of his mind, driven as he was by a strong sense of obligation to the Palestinian people. He was unable to locate any of his own relatives when he traveled to the West Bank, he told me, but had nonetheless felt more at home there than he ever had in his native Santiago. "It was a feeling of great sadness," he explained, "seeing the reality there, but at the same time a feeling of happiness. It's a sense of belonging [*una pertenencia*]. I can't explain it, I can't, I just feel it." When it came to the political potential in his own Palestinianness, he was clear as he echoed a prevalent conviction: "Existence is resistance," he explained. "As long as we exist, that's resistance, because they want to erase us, they want to wipe the Palestinians off the map. So, we keep living. That's resistance."

Meanwhile, although aware that certain others around him saw connections between the situation in Palestine and wider political issues in Chile and abroad, the issue of Palestinian struggle was for Tarek something entirely separated from his perceptions of how things were and should be within his more immediate surroundings.

> I consider myself more right wing, but just when it comes to local politics. I know, for example, that Israel is ultra–right wing with everything they're doing. But yes, I consider myself right wing because I find that the policies that the parties of *la derecha* are trying to implement here are more in line with what I think. For instance, I'm not in favor of free education, I'm not pro-abortion, just to mention a couple of issues. But yes, I condemn the human rights violations that took place under a right-wing government from 1973 until whenever with Pinochet. I completely condemn it, but I also recognize that Pinochet did good things. He allowed us to progress as a country. A lot of people say that being right wing and supporting Palestine are incompatible, but I think those things have nothing to do with each other.

In general, Tarek conceded, he had just never been moved into action by anything other than Palestine. "Look," he told me, "my parents pay for me to go to university. If there was free education [in this country], the truth is that that wouldn't affect me. It's very selfish, yes, but *pucha* [damn], since it doesn't affect me it doesn't move me. Abortion, *pucha*, I'm not in favor of abortion. . . . Marriage equality, I don't care [*me da lo mismo*], so . . . *pucha*." When it came to the Mapuche and the fraught issue of indigenous rights, Tarek's attitude was largely one of uninterest wrapped in his admitted lack of knowledge on the issue. "I don't like to compare the Palestinian cause with the Mapuche. I just feel that they're different," as he put it. Besides, he added, it is difficult to know the truth of the matter without doing serious research. Essentially, he concluded, "there's no way of knowing [*no hay cómo saber*]" enough about the relationship between the Mapuche and the Chilean state to form a proper stance.

Tarek's commitment to remembering Palestine, and to nurturing his sense of belonging to it, seemed easily coupled with his disregard for issues of equality and wider quests for social justice in the context of Chile. He insisted that he had no problem with those whose political views were different from his own and expressed his general contentment that so many people had shown up to commemorate the Nakba and celebrate Palestinian resistance on the evening of the big show in Recoleta, Mapuche flags and all. However, the potential for discord was often an unsettling presence at events gathering disparate voices, both within Palestinian Chilean circles and during times when efforts to remember and call attention to Palestine were brought out into the public realm of the city.

The overall attitude expressed by Tarek appeared somewhat controversial and strangely self-evident all at once. To a busy young man with a lot on his plate, actively engaging in the politics of remembering Palestine and keeping the Palestinian cause ever-present did not seem to leave much room for involvement with other issues. As a consequence, Tarek had decided to stick to what he knew—and what mattered to him personally—and form his politics accordingly. At the same time, as I will describe further in the following chapter, several of Tarek's Palestinian Chilean acquaintances, like Ana and Andrea, found themselves largely unable to simply forget about the political controversies of past and present surrounding them, to the extent that supporting local struggles, such as that of the Mapuche, had become a natural extension of their commitment to Palestine.

For those who experience an ongoing connection with Palestine but go about their daily lives in the context of postdictatorship Chile, there is an ongoing vacillation at play, a tug-of-war between here and there, between one past and another, a vacillation that—to borrow from Ghassan Hage (2009, 77)—has become "a state of being in itself." To them, the struggle over what is remembered—what is allowed visibility and attention—and what is forgotten has become one of the most pressing causes of tension within the realm of the political, although one that is seldom acknowledged as such. Like Tarek, many of those who considered themselves right wing were adamant that all opinions should be welcome and that differing political attitudes should not stand in the way of work being done in support of the Palestinian people. Meanwhile, this seemed more of a strain on those who found themselves unable to commemorate the Nakba without also paying homage to local victims of oppression and critiquing the political structures that have enabled the ongoing reality of inequality in the Chilean context.

In both Chile and Palestine, memory is riddled with politics and remains closely tied to ongoing quests for justice, be they retrospective or prospective. In Santiago, the very sort of memory that is often avoided among Palestinian Chileans poses a counterforce against the burial of the traumatic truths of dictatorship deep in the past, and thus works against the sort of mindful oblivion that to some degree has become characteristic of dealings with issues of memory in postdictatorship (Loveman and Lira 2007; Stern 2010). In turn, the dedication to memory among Palestinian Chileans is a dedication to counter present-day oppression and ongoing displacement in Palestine, a displacement that not only takes place within a physical space but likewise pertains to the realm of time. This paradoxical dynamic between Chilean and Palestinian memory politics, as it plays out within the Palestinian establishment in Santiago, is at the heart of the issues I seek to grapple with in this chapter and in this book as a whole. These issues point especially to one overarching trend: that of ongoing efforts to migrate away from the postmemory of dictatorship into the moving memory of an ongoing chronicle of catastrophe in Palestine and Israel.

For Palestinians, writes Lila Abu-Lughod, "both memory and postmemory have a special valence because the past has not yet passed" (2007, 79). She points to something central not only to the case of Palestinian memory in a general sense, but to the specific dynamics of remembering Palestine in Chile, namely that the past has become a thing of both present and potential future. Hers is without a doubt a poignant observation and one that I do not oppose. I argue, however, that there is more to Palestinian memory than what the concept of postmemory offers. While Huyssen (2003, 3–4) has argued that "the act of remembering is always in and of the present, while its referent is of the past and thus absent," I contend that the referent is not necessarily always of the past. In the present case, the referent's absence is felt in spatial terms, but along the temporal axis it is indeed present, happening in a now that is extended across vast geographical distances. The Nakba remains a watershed moment, but as a mnemonic reference it serves as a point of departure for processes in the present rather than as a fixed and static moment whose place is solely in the past. When people are brought together to commemorate the Nakba, then, they are also brought together in the struggle that has characterized the Palestinian people for decades, that remains unfinished, and that in myriad ways informs and is informed by stories told both in and of the present.

Past and Presence

As mentioned, several events during the week of Nakba commemorations pointed to the continuous nature of the Palestinian catastrophe. A couple of days before the big spectacle in commemoration of the Nakba in Recoleta, I met up with Andrea outside a metro station in the district of Providencia, between downtown Santiago and Las Condes. It was early in the evening, and we were headed to a different kind of show: a lecture on Palestinian memory by a renowned US professor, hosted by the Instituto Chileno-Árabe de Cultura (Chilean-Arab Cultural Institute) and held at the Palestinian Orthodox church nearby. By then Andrea and I had become close and were often accompanying each other to various Palestine-related events. It was without much thought that we had made plans and indeed ended up spending almost every evening during that week together. As we strolled toward the annex next to the church where these sorts of events were often held, Andrea reiterated her commitment to attending as many Nakba ceremonies and happenings as possible and told me she had been rather excited at the prospect of thus reconnecting not only with a bit of history, but with old Palestinian Chilean friends she had been losing touch with, indeed reconnecting with parts of the Palestinian establishment.

Once at the church annex, ten minutes after the event was set to begin, Andrea and I encountered a large room filled to the brim with people, many of whom were still shuffling around trying to make space for a large wooden pew that would add additional seating to the rows of metal folding chairs already in place. The lecture was the second in a series of three given by the professor, all of which had been organized by the University of Chile's Centro de Estudios Árabes, and all of which had turned out to be hugely popular.[13] Once everyone had settled into the hot room, some using their notepads as fans in efforts to fend off the heat, the lecture began. The professor's words came out clearly through a microphone and were being simultaneously translated from English into Spanish and transmitted via headsets hooked up wirelessly to a small translator's box at the far end of the room. Among the audience were many elderly people dressed up for the occasion in suits and dresses, but there were almost as many young people dressed casually in jeans and T-shirts, several of whom were jotting down notes as the lecture and subsequent discussion went on. Palestinian Chilean organizations and groups were well represented, and many of the people I knew from Club Palestino had shown up with friends or family to listen in.

Highlighting the Nakba as an ongoing presence manifesting itself in continuous destruction and disaster, the professor spoke to the current situation in Palestine and likewise brought up the sort of resistance found in refusing to relegate the Nakba to the past and instead continuing to activate it as part of a politics of the present.[14] Indeed, in that sense, the talk became a sort of metanarrative, analyzing the event of commemoration and the act of collective remembrance as it happened. The audience was invited to join in with questions and comments, and after the talk itself, coffee and biscuits were served to keep the conversation going. Andrea, who had been distractedly and impatiently leaning over to scribble little messages and doodle on my notepad during the long talk, took this as a chance to mingle with old friends and acquaintances. To her, although she was not entirely uninterested in scholarly takes on the Palestinian question, this event was first and foremost an opportunity to revive her ties to Palestine as well as the Palestinian sphere in Santiago, something she had begun to do only recently after a long hiatus. At the same time, remembering her connection to Palestine had for Andrea meant reconnecting with the Palestinian struggle. In a move that harked back to her politically active days in the 1980s, she had once again begun wearing her keffiyeh out and about.

By owning Palestinianness in this way, meddling in the way the Palestinian story was told and staged, and indeed insisting on commemorating the Nakba as an unfinished disaster whose presence had moved her to rediscover her keffiyeh along with her political commitment, Andrea and other Palestinian Chileans also claimed ownership of a repertoire of memories that all pertain to an elsewhere. During the Nakba commemorations that took place in Santiago this particular week, the Palestinian past was approached from a variety of angles but always stressing two points: first, that the Nakba is an ongoing catastrophe that cannot yet be left behind, and second, that remembering the Nakba is thus also about remembering what is taking place in Palestine in the present. Be it via musical performances, academic lectures, or solemn commemorative ceremonies, the Nakba was remembered, and continues to be remembered, as a thing of both the past and the present. In that regard, to remember the Palestinian reality in Santiago, I suggest, is also to engage with moving memory—memory in movement, memory that travels in space as well as time. At the same time, it is also to constantly have to negotiate this sort of memory against reminders of past and present realities that some consider worth remembering and others experience as distinctly unmoving and distracting. With that, remembering Palestine is about an engagement that variously foregrounds memory's potential for mobility and immobility, a double potential that is aptly expressed in practices that invite the transfer of memories pertaining to an elsewhere and simultaneously revolve around ever-changing mnemonic barriers.

In this chapter I have begun to grapple with the paradoxical and often tense overlapping relationships with discrete pasts in Santiago—pasts that are by no means "absolute" (Bakhtin 1981, 15). The fractures made visible during Allende's short-lived presidency, and which intensified with the years of military rule and the continued issue of memory in the wake of state violence, have in many ways become defining to present-day Chilean life, and it is these fractures that continue to complicate social life among the capital city's Palestinian Chileans as well as so many other Santiaguinos. The memory at play here is largely characterized by movement: movement between remembrance and oblivion as well as movement within the shadowlands between these outer poles, but also movement across the distance between Palestine and Chile, two nodes within a world shaped by interconnected histories and memories that are increasingly multidirectional and always "more-than-local" (Rothberg 2014, 654).

Much like postmemory, I argue, the connection of moving memory to the past is, in Hirsch's (2008, 107) words, "not actually mediated by recall but by imaginative investment, projection, and creation." Yet because the Zionist project in Palestine stretches out between past and present, this imaginative investment pertains both to memories of the past and knowledge of the present. It is a process through which memories are adopted from an elsewhere, and through which mobilization is tied to these memories. Just as memory transcends simple temporal boundaries, so too can it transcend spatial boundaries. If memories can be adopted from those who lived a reality firsthand in another time, so can they be transferred from another space. At the same time, the term *moving* has another implication. Above, we saw how Tarek felt moved into action for Palestine. To him and many others, commemorating key events such as the Nakba and likewise remembering Palestine in more everyday ways have become central facets of a political commitment as much activated *by* memory as an activator *of* memory (see Gómez-Barris 2015). Conversely, being comfortable enough to forget issues that might be more pressing to others—e.g., Mapuche activists, women dealing with unwanted pregnancies, or students who find themselves unable to pay tuition within Chile's highly privatized sector of higher education—has meant that he simply does not feel moved to get involved in those issues.

In a context where memory remains troublesome, the Palestinian Nakba remains a point of reference for expressions of Palestinianness in Santiago. It is invoked in public discourses as well as private conversations and has in effect become an all-encompassing referent for a continued Palestinian existence in this particular diaspora space (Brah 1996). At the same time, for anyone whose daily life is grounded within the confines of the Chilean state, the ripples of another major event continue to be felt, albeit to varying degrees of intensity or subtlety. Two and a half decades after the Israeli state was founded and forever changed Palestinian life, quotidian existence in Chile underwent drastic changes with Pinochet's entry into the presidential seat at La Moneda. Despite this, Palestinian Chileans often choose to engage in practices of remembrance that are staged to look beyond the near at hand toward an ongoing history of violence and dispossession elsewhere—to engage with memory that moves in more than one sense of the word. Yet this engagement entails attempts to construct boundaries around remembrance. It is these boundaries that will be explored further in the following chapter.

UNEASY ABSENCES

During a conversation with Fernando, a young man in his early twenties who was active in UGEP during the time of my fieldwork, I asked what the Chilean past meant for mobilization around Palestine. He brushed off the issue and simply said he would be happy with any kind of support for the Palestinian cause but did not want Chilean politics to get mixed up in it. Besides, he said, while the violence of dictatorship was awful, Pinochet did Chile a lot of good. This simple statement had come to resound among many of the Palestinian Chileans I knew when I asked them about their take on Chile's troubled past and would become something of a leitmotif as I continued to probe during conversations and interviews. To Fernando, as to many others, the dictatorship era and its effects on current-day Santiago did not seem worth digging into, and my curiosity on the topic was stubbed with talk about Palestine.

In this instance, Fernando reiterated a boiled-down version of Chilean history in which the absence of details with regard to widespread oppression was, perhaps ironically, particularly notable (see Trouillot 1995). The silencing of more disturbing facets of dictatorship was not just characteristic of Fernando's rendition, however, but has rather come to be a constitutive trait of common dealings with memory in postdictatorship. For people like Fernando, two simultaneous processes seemed to be at play. First, the trouble with memory, which still in large part characterizes the relationships of ordinary Chileans with their common past, is no less troublesome for Palestinian Chileans to whom memories of the Pinochet era can be as divisive as they are anywhere. Second, a focus on narratives of the Palestinian past and present within the Palestinian collective sphere in Santiago has meant that memories and postmemories of Chile's recent past have ultimately been pushed aside, at least to the extent possible. The latter process is one that has been stretched out over decades and across various more or less formal institutions. From the Yo Soy Palestino events described in chapter 1 to gaining a more formal education in Palestinianness via Colegio Árabe and various organizations such as UGEP, many of the young Palestinian Chileans I came to know in Santiago have grown up within familial and communal contexts in which people continue to forge long-lasting ties to Palestine, often at the cost of substantial engagement with the details of how Chile has developed as a nation-state in recent decades and beyond. However, as I will return to shortly, the inability to shun and shut out these details as they take the form of material and human reminders often causes frustration. These reminders thus take on irritating qualities (Navaro-Yashin 2012) that turn them into unwelcome presences as they create gray zones where mnemonic boundaries are challenged.

In this chapter I interrogate the everyday ways in which memory constructs, maintains, and feeds off absences that mark an exterior to what is remembered and, as I will return to in chapter 5, made noise about (see Carsten 1995; Stern 2010). In Fernando's take on a past that he, because of his young age, has little chance of remembering firsthand, he makes it clear that some things are worth remembering more than others. In this chapter I argue that he and many others construct and negotiate mnemonic boundaries through a form of "mindful forgetting," which, in the Chilean context, has been conceptualized as a postdictatorship "solution for a dangerously divisive problem without solution" (Stern 2010, 146). If memory holds divisive potential among ordinary Chileans in the era of postdictatorship, this potential, I suggest, takes on another layer of complexity among those whose main concern is with securing presence and unity in the face of struggle elsewhere. However, as intimated above, mnemonic boundaries seldom go unchallenged. More often than not, they are subject to transgressions and partial dismantling by disturbing elements that some would rather have left forgotten. By scrutinizing the production of absences that goes into attempts at managing the past and keeping its disruptive elements at bay, I aim to highlight how approaching memory as *moving* not only helps us point to the related mobile and affective qualities of memory but also allows us to shed light on the inevitable counter to this, namely the ways in which certain facets of the past are deemed void and acted upon as both static and unaffecting. In doing so, I begin to home in on the boundaries, albeit porous, weak, and never fully formed, that come about as a result of the dynamic interplay between moving memory and uneasy absences.

In a country where the main objective among especially state actors seems to have been to look ahead and move on from past strife, forgetting has acquired a central role. According to Brian Loveman and Elizabeth Lira (2007, 44), as part of what has been called *la vía chilena*, a "distinct Chilean way of political reconciliation," efforts to employ a mode of mindful forgetting in order to move forward have been characteristic of Chilean memory work since the nineteenth century. At the same time, the lure of oblivion that exists within certain troubling realms of the past has made its mark on Chileans far and wide, and practices of forgetting have acquired something of a deliberate aspect as a consequence. Without a doubt, the dynamics of oblivion in postdictatorship Chile carry strategic elements, closely linked to the idea of memory as being unconstructive—a drag on the future, as it were (Stern 2010, 149). The relentless back-and-forth between state actors and various grassroots activists about what should be remembered, and how it should be remembered, has been ongoing since the transition to democracy commenced, and the struggle continues as to what sort of memories should be included in the "national emotional glue" and what sort should be subdued (Frazier 2007, 7). At the same time, a certain level of despondency seemed to characterize the relationship between ordinary Chileans and the state and its representatives within and beyond the political establishment during the period of research for this book. This relationship, I suggest, is tightly connected to the ways in which remembrance is practiced and negotiated as a political project in the context of postdictatorship and can shed further light on the dynamics of mnemonic boundary-making.

(Post)dictatorship and Palestine

I often heard complaints that Santiaguinos were not easily pushed to get politically active, and that the outlook of ordinary Chileans was limited at best. During a conversation with Ana, she explained to me how she had reconnected with the Palestinian establishment after years of disengagement. Although she still kept mostly to the fringes, Ana had recently been one of the forces behind a fresh initiative to rally behind the Palestinian cause via different forms of support and advocacy work. As it turned out, this reengagement was directly connected to her perception of the state of Chilean politics. As we sat across from each other at a small wooden table outside a cozy café on a quiet street, Ana pulled her coat closer around her and said, "I always felt included with the Chileans [*los chilenos*] and everything, but always different. My mother always told us we were different." After a sip of her coffee, she went on: "So I guess I always felt included, but there was always a vacuum. And now that I'm participating, that I've been there [Palestine], and most of my friends are Arab, I feel a lot more comfortable." Ana had kept her distance for some time before deciding to join activities at Club

Palestino and elsewhere, but although she had her own grievances about the Palestinian establishment, she saw more of a political commitment among her fellow Palestinian Chileans than elsewhere. To her, taking active part in Palestinian life in the city meant engaging in politics and gaining an international outlook—something she told me she had been missing before. When I asked her what she meant exactly, Ana—echoing the terminology Laila used to describe the Palestinian establishment—explained, "Chile is like a bubble. We're so far away. . . . I think that, geographically speaking, we're in a bubble, and the people here live in a bubble as well. You ask them what's going on in Syria, they have no idea. You ask what's going on in, I don't know, Venezuela, and no one has a clue." Ana had grown tired of what she thought of as a navel-gazing Chilean public and found a springboard into political involvement in a domain dominated by something that to her was distinctly non-Chilean: Palestine and everything Palestinian. Later on, she expanded on her disillusionment with the political climate in her hometown of Santiago. "Here, people don't believe in their own power," she explained. "Chileans want to do things, but they don't know how." Left with little faith in any kind of Chilean politics, establishment or popular, Ana had resorted to supporting *la causa* first and foremost, even though she still felt passionate about the wider implications of her involvement for a politics of potential solidarity. To Ana, disengaging from domestic issues did not mean a lack of interest in the national state of affairs in Chile, but had rather become an expression of despondency in a context where political engagement did not seem to make much of a difference. She was not the first person who had spoken to me of failing initiative, morale, and momentum for political change in the era of postdictatorship. To many of Ana's Palestinian Chilean peers in particular, an overall disenchantment with the political system in Chile had resulted in a move away from domestic issues and deep into a diasporic engagement with Palestine. This move, in turn, was both prompted by and constitutive of what Ana called *bubbles*: distinct spheres made distinct by the boundaries keeping them apart and, I argue, sustained by moving memory.

Somewhat contrary to Ana's perception, of course, many Chileans play a very active role in shaping the political environment of present-day Santiago and beyond, not least since the most recent wave of mass protests set off in late 2019 (see Angell 2007; Escoffier 2014 for similar considerations).[1] Rather than join establishment institutions or organize within political parties, however, many Chileans seem to approach politics through common objectives, and political action often takes on forms not easily matched with established political parties and other institutions.[2] Indeed, the dismantling of authoritarian rule has not lulled the masses by any means. Instead, the era of postdictatorship has seen a remarkable pervasiveness of popular protest in various forms; all the while, traditional political parties are being abandoned (see also Garretón [1989] 2001; Sehnbruch and Donoso 2011). That this should be the case not only has to do with the legacy and ramifications of military rule and the subsequent return to democracy but also points to pervasive corruption scandals and a class of politicians and technocrats who seem largely unable to inspire confidence among the electorate (Roberts 2012). Already in the mid-to-late 1990s, argues Steve Stern (2010, 192), a certain "disgust with politics as a kind of fiction" characterized the mood in postdictatorship Chile, where people began to look elsewhere for meaning and purpose. Since then, a lack of confidence in and involvement with political parties and other established political institutions has only become ever more pronounced in Santiago and beyond. Although this tendency is thus very much a thing of the present, it cannot be separated from the country's tumultuous past. Indeed, it has been argued, much of the discouragement from political participation experienced in postdictatorship was initially spurred on by "the notion that 'politicization' was to blame for the coup" (Elsey 2011, 251). Further, according to Gómez-Barris (2009, 33), the very trauma of dictatorship produced "an impossibility of reattachment to national projects." Despite of a lack of attachment to establishment—or what Gómez-Barris calls national—projects, a significant portion of Santiaguinos continue to mobilize and act on their own.

Rather than a newfound democracy, what the citizens of Chile were offered in the wake of Pinochet's exit was an extended period of transition from dictatorship to democratic rule. As Stern (2010, 126) writes, the "victory of the No in the 1988 plebiscite on continuation of Pinochet's rule . . . created not a democracy, but a democratic opening."[3] Postdictatorship Chile is, as such, in a continuous state of *post*, of not yet having surpassed the events of the past. In other words, the past has not entirely been put behind, and the dragged-out process of return to democracy attests to the still lingering effects of dictatorship on the present. In that sense, Chileans continually face the "*afterlife* of political violence" in Chile—an afterlife marked by the continuous "wrestling with the past in the present" (Gómez-Barris 2009, 6; italics in the original). It is not difficult to imagine that, when dictatorship came to an end, "a persistent range of ethical and political divisions about the interpretation of the past survived" (Lira 2011, 108). The past has not only remained present in the current state of inequality within Chilean society, but also in the diverging views on that very past—views that continue to diverge and collide as memory initiatives and collective efforts at coming to terms with the events of the last few decades wax and wane. While memory was to become a huge theme in postdictatorship Chile, however, the early days of democratic transitioning have generally been depicted as being marked by the compulsion to forget and to effectively block out the years of military rule (see

Moulian in Gómez-Barris 2009, 4). Perhaps paradoxically, early efforts to reckon with the past were part of this wider tendency. As Gómez-Barris (2009, 25) argues, testimony and truth-seeking efforts became part of a quest to bury the past in the past and to move on into Chile's new democracy, with reconciliation becoming "a form of concealment." In the early 1990s, however, the memory issue was "at once a moral, political, and even existential question" (Stern 2010, 125). If these observations seem discrepant, it is simply that they reflect the trouble with memory in Chile after Pinochet. Struggles between forces who would have the past play no part in the present and those who seem intent on continued remembrance and reckoning still constitute a major fault line in Chilean society.

Of course, Palestinian Chileans were impacted as much as the rest of the country's population by military rule and its consequences. Take, for example, UGEP. In the late 1980s, in the early years after the Chilean chapter of the organization was formed, its members made themselves noticed in Pinochet's Santiago by wearing their keffiyehs proudly on the street. As related by Andrea, who was active in UGEP back then, she and the other members demonstrated their connection to the Palestinian cause in this way, only to be called communists, *turcos*, and terrorists by strangers passing them by (see also Lira 2011, 115). The UGEP of the Pinochet years was clearly marked by a national political context in which showing support for the Palestinian cause, for many, meant showing support for the communist movement in Chile and thus resistance to the dictatorship (see Jadue 2014).

When I asked Andrea if UGEP back then was actually against Pinochet and military rule, her response was a prompt "of course!" Indeed, especially for Andrea, the Palestinian cause became a way to deal with and understand her frustration with the regime. As she put it, "I had to arrive at the Palestinian cause in the end because before [discovering] the Palestinian cause I didn't understand the injustice [of dictatorship]. . . . I just knew I couldn't stand this guy [Pinochet] on TV saying 'you have to do this' and 'you have to do that.'" Of course, many Palestinian Chileans experienced those years very differently from Andrea, but whatever people's attitude to Pinochet and the junta—as was described to me by several people—all politics seemed at that time to be entangled in the politics of dictatorship, and any show of solidarity within or beyond Chilean state borders was perceived to carry a sort of subversive quality, potentially posing a threat to the way things were. At the same time, for many of those young UGEPers of the 1980s who did not support Pinochet, mobilizing around other causes far removed from the center of Chilean politics in Santiago indeed became a way to, perhaps not too subtly, express discontent with the local lay of the land. Since the end of military rule, however, the borders between Chilean and Palestinian (memory) politics seem to have become more starkly drawn.

Alex was a young man of twenty-five, ambitious and academically inclined, whom I had come to know as highly engaged in Palestinian circles, but who at the same time often had an air of detachment about him. During one conversation we had, Alex told me about growing up Palestinian in the context of postdictatorship: "The eighteenth of September, the independence of Chile, *las fiestas patrias*, is also my grandfather's birthday, so every year on the eighteenth of September my cousins would play Arab music, and I learned to play too, thanks to them. The eighteenth of September, until I was about fifteen, was always celebrated with Arab music, Arab food, *cachai* [you know]? And I think that for that reason I have this strong sense of being Palestinian." Alex's memories of childhood holidays spent celebrating his grandfather rather than the founding fathers of the Chilean state are illuminating of the process, common among the people I knew in Santiago, by which the Chilean is oftentimes put aside and forgotten for the sake of the Palestinian. Though Alex's is a special case—not all Palestinian Chileans have family members whose birthdays fall on national holidays—it speaks volumes about a dynamic that is usually more subtle. The practice of foregrounding the Palestinian while disregarding the Chilean reflects both a certain unease at engaging with the past and present of a troubled state, and the importance awarded to continuous commitment to the matter of Palestine—past, present, and future.

This memory dynamic is grounded in a history of migration, but as Sara Ahmed (1999, 342) notes, "migration is not only felt at the level of lived embodiment" but "is also a matter of generational acts of story-telling about prior histories of movement and dislocation." Following this, Alex's childhood celebrations might be understood as a continuous movement—not simply a sort of migration away from the Chilean reality and into the mnemonic reality of Palestine, but rather as an ongoing vacillation between spaces and times. Rather than engaging in a sort of postmemory of dictatorship, then, Alex took part in a form of familial memory work that referred not only to a different past, but to a different place altogether. As Alex's mnemonic movement from the—in physical terms—present Chile to the absent Palestine so strikingly shows, the "post" in postdictatorship does not necessarily imply that memory in this context should likewise imply postmemory, at least for some. Instead, as Alex was moved by memories of celebrating an elsewhere, he also continuously kept these memories in motion.

Alex's story of how his family used to spend the *fiestas patrias* during his childhood in the 1990s is not only interesting in that it foregrounds how memory sometimes refers to faraway places. It is also a pertinent example of subtle resistance to a celebratory kind of postdictatorship memory. Especially in the early years of military rule, because the national *fiestas patrias* coincided with the anniversary of the coup on September 11, mid-September became something of a new "memory season" (Stern 2010, 38). Designed by Pinochet and his allies to pay tribute to the alleged heroes of the "second independence of 1973," commemorations around this time of year bore an unsettling, at least for some, sense of complicity in the violence of dictatorship, giving many a reason to shy away from any form of involvement in the festivities (Stern 2010, 38).

The three cases described above foreground different nuances to a story of movement from Chilean memory politics to Palestinian. What the narratives above have in common, however, is the commitment to remembering an *elsewhere* within the context of a *here* that poses a number of challenges. To Ana, it was a general sense of despondency and disenchantment with Chilean politics that spurred her to become involved with the Palestinian establishment; to Andrea, both during dictatorship and since then, a political commitment to *la causa* allowed her to contextualize and articulate her experiences of discontent under military rule; and to Alex, the family tradition of celebrating his grandfather and, with him, all things Palestinian on the eighteenth of September became a way to ensure a certain distance from a complex and highly politicized national holiday with all its contentious connotations. By focusing their energies on the politics of remembering Palestinian traditions and struggles, Ana, Andrea, and Alex have all in their own way taken part in creating absences around complex (post)dictatorship politics, effectively practicing a kind of mindful forgetting. However, as all three were well aware, the cleavages thus created between bundles of memory politics remain flexible and easily bridged. Indeed, while they were moved by Palestinian memory, they also recognized a potential for Palestinian memory politics to *move something* more locally—Andrea through a subtle form of keffiyeh-borne protest, Alex through a familial disapproval of a Pinochet-celebrating "memory season," and Ana through her attention, albeit still non-materialized, to ways in which her work for Palestine might have an effect closer to home.

Unwelcome Presences

A mnemonic migration similar to the one described above can be detected among Palestinian Chilean individuals and families that both gained from and supported the junta's lengthy rule. For them, the Pinochet years were seen as a blessing to both themselves and the wider Palestinian establishment. Many of them traders and entrepreneurs, as described in chapter 1, Palestinians and their descendants in Chile—and perhaps especially those with well-established businesses in Patronato and other parts of the capital city—benefited greatly from the neoliberal policies of the 1970s and '80s. Indeed, many continue to believe that military rule rescued a Chile on the brink of disaster and set the country on the right course (see Stern 2010, 109).[4] Whereas this might have been the case among a wide range of Pinochet's supporters in the early years of postdictatorship, and perhaps still is, it is something that most often remains unspoken within Palestinian Chilean circles. While some remain vocal about their support for Pinochet's political project, most have opted to leave their enthusiasm unspoken and simply embrace the changes that have resulted from dictatorship-era policies. Postdictatorship memory is neither celebratory nor mournful for them; it is rather to a great extent absent.

A couple of months before my conversation with Fernando, I joined Laila at her university on the northeast outskirts of the city for a walk through the campus. Around this time, the annual UGEP leadership elections were coming up, and both Laila and I were preoccupied with what might happen. After a stroll around the large campus, we sat down on one of the benches scattered throughout the grounds, where green lawns were sprinkled with little knolls and corners of shade. We had already toured the main building, eerily empty before the start of the term, and had come back outside from one of the modern concrete structures to get some air. Our conversation quickly turned to the topic of the UGEP elections. Candidates for the organization's executive committee (*directiva*) had already been campaigning for some time, hoping to win one of the five positions available, and tension seemed to be building as competition got fiercer. During the time I had already spent within UGEP, I had noted a mostly subtle rivalry between certain UGEP members. On several occasions before, Laila had conceded that the UGEP leadership and core group had two informal blocs: one conservative and the other more left-leaning. The notion that UGEP was a political and yet nonideological organization had been repeated to me by many and was not perceived to point to any tensions worth dwelling on. When I approached the topic with Laila, she brushed it off with a sweep of the hand and a quick comment: "We want a free Palestine, we don't care about the left or right. . . . We know how to keep things separate." At the same time, I knew Laila was concerned with the elections and was hoping that one of her conservative friends from the group would manage to get enough votes to win the chairmanship.

That political stances beyond Palestine could mean so little and so much at the same time did not appear to seem incongruous in the slightest to Laila or the rest of UGEP. Indeed, while political attitudes and friendship alliances seemed to overlap within the core group, not a word on ideology or domestic politics had ever been spoken during any of the meetings and events I had attended with them. These gatherings were not always free of conflict and tension, but arguments never referred to opposing political views and seemed rather to center on specific tasks and interpersonal quarrels. At the same time, both formal and informal UGEP gatherings had an air of affection, of friendship, and of a tight-knit social fabric within a group of old friends who simply happened to not always agree on everything.

Later on, however, the issue was further complicated. A few months after our tour of her university, Laila had summoned me and a mutual friend for lunch along with Tarek. After collecting Tarek at his house on the way, we all drove east in Laila's car and ended up in a fast-food restaurant in Las Condes. Although there was a sense of tiredness to the group and conversation was a bit slow, the issue of the ongoing mobilization around Gaza quickly came up. By this time Operation Protective Edge had kicked off, and everyone seemed to be feeling the weight of the violence in Gaza. Tarek seemed particularly frustrated and approached the conversation with a noncommittal frown otherwise rather unlike him. As we sat around a red plastic table and ate our pizza straight from its cardboard box, however, he started opening up. Once he got talking, Tarek emphatically expressed his irritation at what he perceived as fragmentation within the Palestinian establishment. To him, organizations and groups that had sprung up as a result of the current crisis were illegitimate and failed to act within the widest possible consensus among Palestinian Chileans. He mentioned in particular a new group, which he said had been formed completely independently by "some guy" who didn't think UGEP was doing enough.

This person, Tarek explained, was indeed *palestino* but not really part of the establishment and therefore considered an outsider. Even worse, it appeared from Tarek's expression as he continued, this outsider just seemed "too caught up" in left-wing politics. An uncomfortable ambivalence marked much of Tarek's involvement in marches and other forms of political mobilization that reached beyond the realm of Club Palestino and the Palestinian establishment. Independent groups and organizations had started acting without seeking the support of UGEP or the Federation, and Tarek felt that the more established and well-respected institutions were being slighted. Not only that, but the emergence of these groups also meant that attention was being redirected from Palestine and scattered among a host of other issues, in effect turning the Palestinian struggle and the crisis in Gaza into a mere backdrop for the promotion of what both Tarek and Laila considered irrelevant politics.

A few weeks earlier, the first in a range of demonstrations against the assault on Gaza had taken place in the city. Now, as he thought back to it, Tarek's frustration was evident. The protest had been planned in cooperation between various groups and organizations, but some of them had gone rogue during the event and started an unauthorized march, which went beyond the plan that had been approved by city authorities. Moreover, Tarek complained, he had practically had to fight for the megaphone to be able to speak for UGEP among an array of other speakers, many of whom had strayed from the topic and brought up other issues, namely the Mapuche struggle and the current challenges faced by the Chilean student movement. Indeed, there had perhaps been a certain discrepancy between the stated purpose of the demonstration and the messages that had been yelled out through the megaphone as speakers scrambled to have their voices heard on the makeshift stage. What did seem to tie these messages together, however, was the recurring theme of solidarity and the not very subtle inclination among most speakers for a distinct *izquierda* politics.

When I followed up on this conversation with Laila some time later, she delved directly into the tension that Tarek seemed to be speaking to as he had voiced his frustration at meddling speakers and rogue organizers. "They always say that UGEP and the Federation are political but don't pick sides," Laila started. "And they've always said that they don't care about party politics, and they don't want to tie themselves to one side." At the same time, she explained, reality looks a bit different from the absolute neutrality professed from within these organizations where conservatism is widespread. Indeed, she conceded, many of her fellow UGEP members and other Palestinian Chilean peers had expressed dismay at the presence of people carrying communist banners or Mapuche flags at pro-Palestine marches, blatantly wearing their own politics on their sleeve. But, Laila said, "I've never understood why there's a problem with the communists if *la derecha* doesn't do anything. It's like we're waiting for the day when *la derecha* will see and support us, but they haven't shown up yet."

Despite statements to the contrary, among people like Laila and Tarek the idea of solidarity across issues or causes seemed to make them uneasy and irritated— even if waiting around for *la derecha* to show up did not exactly seem like a useful alternative to tolerating the presence of communists and Mapuche. At the same time, the current politics of both those groups and others connected with *la izquierda* were and still are indelibly tied to a traumatic past that has produced seemingly irreparable tears in the fabric of Chilean memory. Among the young people of UGEP and within the wider realm of institutionalized Palestinian Chilean life, then, grievances arose when the Palestinian cause got mixed up with struggles that, to some, were not easily paired with it and that, perhaps more important, seemed upsetting—in the widest sense of the word—in all their complexity.

Within the context of the Palestinian establishment in Santiago, both communists and Mapuche have often come to act as reminders of an uncomfortable past and still present political struggles, and their presence at marches and other events was met with feelings of unease, frustration, and a general sense of irritation. Navaro-Yashin defines irritability as a "dis-resonating feeling produced by environments that harbor phantoms" (2012, 20). In this case, not only does the landscape of the city harbor ghostly traces of disturbing pasts, so too do the human bodies whose uninvited and unwelcome presences disrupt an otherwise clearly demarcated and focused protest against unfinished colonial violence elsewhere. Despite a prevalent desire for mindful forgetting, then, attempted boundary-making in the realm of memory politics is often met with counterefforts to find common ground and act in mutual solidarity, much to the frustration of certain people.

Defying Erasure, Erasing Defiance

Writing on Palestinian families in Denmark, Anja Kublitz (2011) argues that absences and silences create a gap through which the Palestinian struggle can be appropriated to fit the present. In these families, Kublitz asserts, the past comes through in fragments of silences and absences as much as words and actions. Certain stories, specific events, and aspects of war are simply left out of parents' historical narratives in the family setting. However, in Kublitz's view, what is not being said—the silence—speaks volumes; although the specifics of the past remain unarticulated, the physical absence of a homeland leaves the children acutely aware of past circumstances that spill over into the present. With the particularities of the past silenced, however, the young people in Kublitz's case find a space to transform the Palestinian struggle into a kind of struggle that fits their reality in Copenhagen, a reality marked by experiences of discrimination, a War on Terror, and discourses that juxtapose Muslims and the West. The Palestinian struggle is thus molded by them in the space made available by the silences and absences that permeate daily life within the families.

Among Palestinian Chileans in Santiago there are few memories of war and Israeli violence to silence. As opposed to the Palestinian families in Copenhagen that Kublitz writes about, Palestinian Chilean families and organizations in Santiago go to great lengths to articulate a past and current Palestinian struggle in details that, for the most part, are known to them only through the accounts of others. Here, a different set of silences, which pertain to the local context, are at play. Through the mindful forgetting and active muting of a troubled Chilean past, people like those mentioned in these pages are able to mold their collective experiences and endeavors around a type of memory that unifies rather than separates. By thus making a mnemonic move from one past to another, Palestinian Chileans manage, at least to an extent, to prevent ruptures in and disruptions to their joint political project. As we have seen, however, the reality of memory politics in Santiago is complex, and conflicts between opposed memories cannot always be kept at bay. Despite efforts to create boundaries around it, Palestinian

Chilean memory does not exist apart from its surroundings but takes up its own little corner in the memory world of postdictatorship. Both a long Palestinian history of struggle and an intricate and long history of Palestinian migration to Chile continuously affect social dynamics in and beyond the diasporic establishment. At the same time, as pointed out, Palestinian memory has, in the broad sense, become one measure by which to counteract ongoing efforts to deny Palestinians a physical, symbolic, and historical presence. Forming a coherent set of countermemories on Palestine has indeed become a political endeavor (see Abu-Lughod and Sa'di 2007, 6).

Despite opposing views on memory after military rule, an era of reckoning commenced with the transition from dictatorship to democracy that was set into motion with the 1988 plebiscite. Efforts to confront this period of simultaneous violence, prosperity, development, and suppression were put in gear immediately following Pinochet's exit as head of state, but legislation granting amnesty to the general's accomplices had been implemented already during the period of dictatorship (see, e.g., Gómez-Barris 2009; Stern 2010). In that way, Pinochet and those who worked with him had made sure to proactively hinder memory work from turning into legal prosecution after the years of military rule had come to an end.[5] However, on October 16, 1998, Pinochet was arrested in London on charges of crimes against humanity, following an extradition request from Spain (see Paley 2001, 1; Sorensen 2011, 159). While the arrest was celebrated internationally, the Chilean government saw the event as potentially disturbing for the transition to democracy. The concern of the Chilean government on the matter of Pinochet, who had by then been appointed lifetime senator, and his apprehension in London speaks volumes about the continued vulnerability of the new democracy, as well as the deep disagreements that prevailed on the subjects of memory and justice (see Wood 1999, 198).[6]

At the same time, Pinochet's arrest caused strong emotional reactions among people back in Chile, as did his death in 2006. Andrea related to me how, after a stint abroad, she had returned to Santiago just a few days after Pinochet's death to find her family in an uproar. While attending a family dinner at her mother's house, Andrea, who had been happy to see the end of the dictator, had gotten into a heated argument with her mother and brothers, all of whom had supported Pinochet. "I was so happy he was gone," she explained. "Everyone had been so brainwashed by him. My mother was crying, my brothers yelling at me. . . . Just imagine [*imagínate*], everyone thought that there was going to be a crisis after Pinochet died. They were scared there was going to be a civil war . . . but nothing happened." According to Andrea, her conservative family members had been worried that Pinochet's death would somehow result in a massive uprising led by those who had opposed him, assuming that they had only stayed quiet because he was still around. However, as Andrea pointed out, things did not go as badly as her family had imagined. Meanwhile, the death of the former dictator did leave marks on the family dynamic. "They're all nuts!" she told me. "We just can't talk about this issue in my family anymore." When I asked Andrea what the issue of Pinochet and military rule had meant for the Palestinian establishment, she promptly responded, "It divides us. The right-wing [Palestinian Chileans] are just completely brainwashed. I can't discuss this with them." For Andrea, her relationships to both close family and wider community had become marked by mnemonic boundaries across which communication seemed pointless. Not only had a boundary been established between left-wing and right-wing memory respectively, but also between Palestinian memory, celebrated and kept alive, and Chilean memory, contentious and therefore kept still. To return to Laila's and Ana's apt image, memory had been organized by these boundaries into distinct bubbles. This was also a large part of the reason Andrea had kept her distance from the Palestinian establishment for a prolonged period before I met her.

The constant push-and-pull between past and future seems characteristic of the Chilean nation-state in which practices of mindful forgetting are commonplace, as the recent past keeps a tight grip on both personal and political relationships. Yet while the subject of Pinochet and fraught memories of military rule cannot easily be dealt with within the domain of the Palestinian establishment—and in some cases, within Palestinian Chilean families—memories pertaining to the ongoing Palestinian struggle, and in particular the Nakba, are regularly brought forth without conflict. Ambivalence and unease, however, mark the relationships of many to Chile's troubled past and its reminders.

In all their varying points of departure and diverse ideological stances, everyone mentioned here moved on the same mnemonic playing field during the time I spent with them. Their attitudes toward Chilean memory in postdictatorship, although quite dissimilar at the surface level, are illuminating of a broader tendency to practice memory politics in relation to movement or lack thereof. Again, it becomes clear how moving memory works at several levels. It covers the ways in which memories travel and are transplanted spatially from an elsewhere; it points us to the affective qualities of memory; and it alerts us to the political potential in maintaining momentum in both respects. The corollary to this, of course, is that people tend to ensure this momentum in part by working to keep other pasts still and immobile through practices of mindful forgetting that create mnemonic absences. These absences do not necessarily stay absent for long, but rear their heads in the shape of unwelcome and irritating presences, of communists and Mapuche, and even sometimes in the shape of attitudes that cause friction within families.

In Chile as much as elsewhere, memory is not only troubled, but also continuously troubling. Unsurprisingly, not least in this case, silences and absences are both inevitable and important aspects of memory politics. Particularly within the Palestinian establishment in Santiago, the erosion of memory is perhaps most clearly seen with young people who have had to rely on accounts and narratives of dictatorship passed down via those who lived through it (see Augé 2004). As the examples above show, forgetting can indeed be mindful, and oblivion a strategic practice that serves to demarcate present and moving memories of an elsewhere from memories that could be upsetting in a number of ways and that indeed, as we just saw, *are* upsetting when attempts fail to keep them at bay. Mindful forgetting is not just about leaving behind particular facets or certain versions of the past. It is indeed about making an effort to cut oneself off from the imposing memory politics of others. What remains of memory is often both struggled for and tied to a politics that is at once filled with resistance and purpose, both for Palestinian Chileans and for those communists, Mapuche, and others whom they often want nothing to do with.

In that context, efforts to silence other pasts and wishes for the invisibility and absence of their irritating reminders not only reinforce—in highly flawed and largely unsuccessful ways—existing social and political boundaries, but also risk making invisible the forces of oppression that have shaped these pasts and that continue to have an impact on real people living real lives. Stoler has highlighted the role of occlusion as it "hides and conceals, creates blockage, and closes off" colonial histories of the present (2016, 10). In line with her concern regarding the ways in which our colonial pasts are subject to acts of obstruction, I want to highlight how moving memory can be used to occlude what lies beyond it, producing relations centered on stillness, stagnation, and mutual *unmoving* between certain pasts and the people who do not immediately recognize them as their own. In the case of remembering Palestine, using memory as a tool to defy erasure elsewhere has come to entail an ongoing albeit never total erasure of defiance in the face of oppression faced locally and in the wake of particular histories of globally interlinked patterns of violence.[7] The mnemonic boundaries, however, that separate the visible from the invisible, noise from silence, and moving from still are porous and unstable from the outset and continually disrupted by presences that some may consider unwelcome, but that are nonetheless reluctantly summoned.

Between Afterlives of Violence

As central to political storytelling as the watershed moments of the Nakba of 1948 and the coup of 1973 have been to the Palestinian and Chilean nations respectively, they are by no means approached on equal terms within the Palestinian establishment in Santiago. While the Nakba remains a recurring theme in political, historical, and indeed familial narratives within Palestinian Chilean circles, the coup of 1973 and the years of dictatorship that followed are often met with unease, ambivalence, and frustration. Rather than a highly contentious and potentially divisive issue, the Palestinian past is a prominent and welcome part of the communal realm and is told and retold time and again through a process that continues to reconfigure the reality of the diasporic Palestinian experience, past and present. The era of Chilean dictatorship, meanwhile, has come to bear little relevance to the sort of everyday life that is most often centered on an elsewhere. Especially among young Palestinian Chileans who did not live through the years of military rule—or who were too young to remember—the tensions that remain around the issue of memory in wider Chilean society can indeed become a bit of a nuisance, and something it seems better to just forget about. At the same time, a strategically tinged forgetting within the Palestinian establishment in Santiago is a practice that bares its relevance primarily when directly tied to the realm of community. As individuals, many Palestinian Chileans remain well aware that their political views might differ from those of their families, friends, and peers. The awareness of potential ruptures, however, is toned down, intentionally it seems, and with thorough consideration, in contexts where the more pressing issue of Palestine is at stake.

Oblivion is not necessarily always welcomed, but seems always to link to larger struggles, in Chile and beyond. For most Palestinian Chileans born during military rule, lived memory circles around the experiences of a Santiago marked by postdictatorship and is far removed from the everyday intricacies of violence in Palestine. But is memory lived necessarily memory alive? What I have tried to show in this chapter is that that does not seem to be the case. To a certain extent, of course, the history of dictatorship-era Chile is transmitted to those who did not live it, through family accounts as much as dominant public narratives at the local and national level; but at the same time, silences and shifting narratives interplay to make for an uneven mnemonic playing field, as it were. There seems to be little consensus, even now, on how the time of dictatorship and the subsequent democratic opening should be approached and thought of, both among those who were alive and aware at the time and those whose entire relationship with this past is based on the narratives of others. The history of Chile from the late 1960s until today is still being written, and it is doubtful that any one version will ever be considered the ultimate truth. While many engage in more or less strategic practices of mindful forgetting, others remain caught up in a tense struggle between those who still seek recognition of their memories and those who advocate oblivion—the quest for remembrance often implying a quest for justice. In either case, both remembrance and oblivion are practices that are often undertaken with a particular goal in mind.

In this chapter, I have scrutinized the uneasy absences that come about as people mindfully try to forget disturbing pasts. These absences are often doubly uneasy: they create discomfort in their never-complete nonappearance and prove difficult to maintain as absences at the same time. In interrogating these absences, I have paid particular attention to the irritating qualities of presences produced by those who refuse to let their stories of struggle stay muted and hidden from plain view. Memories that move—both geographically and affectively speaking—are memories alive, in that sense, while memories that are (kept) still wither and slowly die. In approaching memory as moving, it follows that forgetting entails a lack of movement. As a lived phenomenon, however, remembrance rarely works in such neatly conceptualized ways, although some might like it to be otherwise. Rather, maintaining moving memories and the boundaries that ostensibly protect them from disturbing elements requires constant negotiation and is a forever incomplete labor.

Memory is both manifested and negotiated in myriad ways within myriad settings. While memory as practice, and indeed memory as narrative, are important aspects of contemporary memory politics, they do not stand apart from memory's other facets. Rather, these practices and narratives are tightly bound to the spaces within which they, to use an appropriate expression, *take place*. As Jonathan Boyarin (1994, 20) phrases it, "memory erupts into and shapes" space in "often ambiguous ways." In turn, it might be added, spatial manifestations of memory work to shape memory itself, along with the practices and narratives that go with it. It is these spatial manifestations that will be scrutinized in the following chapter, with a particular focus on Club Palestino as a locus of remembrance.

WHERE MEMORY MOVES

On a sunny day in late spring, Club Palestino is teeming with life. Children are splashing around in the pool or queuing up to go on the waterslide or to jump in from one of the tall springboards. Meanwhile, families and groups of friends have set up camp nearby on the grass, sitting on blankets or large, colorful towels. Laila and a couple of other UGEP members hang around in bathing suits on a small knoll overlooking the pool area, soaking up the sun while carefully putting together colorful beads on pieces of string—slow, meticulous work that will provide them with extra goods to sell at the club's annual Gran Bazaar, where they will be raising funds for their work. The activity on the tennis courts at the southern edge of the club can be heard in the distance, hollow thumps coming across at regular intervals as rackets and tennis balls collide. The sound of playing children, however, dominates, not least when they come running up to the deeply focused UGEPers to interrupt and ask curiously what they are working on, ice cream dripping from their hands onto the grass. Within a compound protected by walls and gates, the only intrusions from the outside world on what is going on by the pool and on the tennis courts are the low hum of traffic from the busy road behind the parking lot and the sight of apartment buildings that lead the eye further toward the protruding Andes mountains to the east, partly covered in a haze of smog that leaves them otherwise fairly easily forgotten. On this day the club is first and foremost a place for basking in the sun with family and friends and for taking a dip in the pool if so inclined. Meanwhile, as on all other occasions, the place is marked by a sense of containment and offers no visible hints that its history bears traces of significant entanglements with a dictatorial regime that yielded prosperity among many of the club's users and neighbors. Club Palestino is a place where Palestine is always kept present but where the outside world is kept at a distance by mnemonic occlusion as much as by metal gates.

With Club Palestino as its entry point, this chapter interrogates the tensions inherent in what I call the city's mnemonic landscape and scrutinizes the relationships between memory, oblivion, and place making. In it, I argue that Club Palestino, as a place located at the junction of two discrete and yet interlinked histories of oppression and dissent, not only continues to evolve as a node in the built environment of postdictatorship Santiago but is constantly undergoing negotiation as a site of both remembrance and oblivion, a spatial extension of wider struggles with and for memory. The recent past and the memories that in various and often conflicting ways refer to it are central facets of the human geography of Santiago, and of Club Palestino as part of it. These ultimately make for an uneven mnemonic landscape that emanates disparate stories and thus directs our attention to the multivocality of the past as a highly contested present phenomenon (Foote and Azaryahu 2007; Foucault 1986; Massey 1995). In other words, the complexity that lends the city its texture is bound to contesting politics and ongoing efforts to steer the realities of the past and present toward certain visions of the future. According to Gunnar Maus, "a landscape of memory consists of several *bundles* of practices of memory and their corresponding commemorative arrangements. It is an abstract conception of the pastness of our world that is constituted in routinised practices of localised memory and anchored at specific places" (2015, 218; italics in the original). What I call the mnemonic landscape can be thought of similarly, but what I want to highlight here is how the bundles of practices and materializations of memory that constitute it sometimes clash with and challenge each other, thus making the landscape as such inherently contentious and filled, in turn, with bundles of silences (Trouillot 1995). In this chapter, I treat Club Palestino and the activities that take place within it as one such bundle: a bundle that adds to the texture of the wider mnemonic landscape in Santiago but, I argue, ultimately supports its order by creating physical and social, albeit malleable, borders around itself as a Palestinian place.

Club Palestino and Its Reminders

The landscape of northeastern Santiago tells of relative wealth and rapid development. It belongs to a twenty-first-century Chile that has consolidated the neoliberal politics that came to characterize the last few decades of the century before. Not only is this new Santiago ripe with shopping malls, shiny restaurants, and US café and fast-food chains. Even the streets, the sidewalks, and the parks in the districts of Las Condes, Vitacura, and much of Providencia almost seem to have a certain shine to them, modern infrastructural constructions as they are. In glassy apartments far above the ground or in villas behind security gates and barbed wire on quiet streets in Las Condes, many Palestinian Chilean families have made this part of Santiago their home, while others continue to reside in more modest dwellings elsewhere.

A different kind of Palestinian home is located here, too. Club Palestino lies at the northern edge of Las Condes, right at the border to neighboring Vitacura. The heavily trafficked Avenida Presidente Kennedy solidly places the club within Las Condes territory, however, while a tall and thick redbrick wall marks the perimeter of the club and shelters its users from the worst of the traffic noise. To get beyond the wall a visitor must enter—either by car or by foot—through metal gates guarded by security personnel who are usually friendly and familiar with most of those who come through. On the wall next to these gates, big golden letters spell out CLUB PALESTINO, while just behind these letters, on the other side of the wall, two protruding flagpoles fly the Chilean and the Palestinian flags next to each other, making it almost impossible for outsiders to mistake this place for anything but a Palestinian Chilean institution.

Meanwhile, a different type of message is communicated at the gates of Club Palestino; also behind the wall, at a short distance from the flags and the golden letters, a massive billboard—so tall that it is sure to catch the eye of anyone driving past the club on the large avenue in front—features seven capitalized letters in black, red, and green: GAZAMOR. A play on the words Gaza and *amor*, the message is clear: Gaza needs love. Below is an even clearer message to those who look more closely: "Palestina necesita tu ayuda"—Palestine needs your help. Under the billboard, a large banner is stretched out, its bottom edge resting on top of the brick wall. Flanked by the Chilean and the Palestinian flags at either end, a similar message is spelled out in black letters on a white background: "Fin a la ocupación: paz en Palestina"—End the occupation: peace in Palestine. These signs not only mark the entrance to a Palestinian place, but alert visitors to the particular message that resides here and that extends itself beyond the gates.

All year round, Club Palestino lends its turf to a wide range of events and activities. One of its main functions is as a sports club, and the tennis courts are only one of many sports facilities within the compound. At the same time, it is a place for socializing, with cafés and lounges available for get-togethers both big and small. The large park that takes up most of the property includes extensive grassy fields, a pool area, a playground, and countless paths, nooks, and crannies. Besides the main building, several other constructions lie scattered about and are used for various purposes, the most impressive being the relatively large gymnasium that borders one of the big parking lots within the compound for easy access. Beyond sports and socializing, however, Club Palestino is a place for organizing and mobilizing efforts for Palestine. It is where most UGEP meetings take place and where the Federation has its headquarters. Likewise, it is where conferences and congresses are held and where campaigns are planned and prepared for—envelopes licked, donation boxes decorated, banners and signs painted, and medicine for Gaza sorted and packed before being shipped off.

As a hub of Palestinian life in Santiago, Club Palestino is without a doubt a place intimately connected with both Palestine and the Palestinian struggle in ways that I will return to shortly. It is also a place of politics. The signs visible to outsiders passing the club on the road in front are but one telltale sign that Palestine is high on the agenda here. Inside the gates, Club Palestino is filled with signifiers that point to a certain rootedness in a reality far from Santiago. At a crossroads in the narrow paths that cut through the landscape, a lamppost supports metal signs in the shape of arrows pointing in different directions. *Tenis*, reads one of them, with the Arabic translation written next to the Spanish word. Pointing in a slightly different direction, another arrow guides the visitor toward *fútbol*, while a third sign simply reads "*Palestina*, فلسطين (falastin), 13.224 km." Meanwhile, the main building, perched at the far end of a path laid out in stone tiles from the gate, is replete with material objects that tell of the connection of this place to Palestine. On the other side of the large wooden doors, in the cool interior of the building, Palestinian images are omnipresent. Paintings depicting dark-haired women in headscarves intermix with various plaques on the walls, and in the main meeting room on the ground floor, a photograph of Palestinian president Mahmoud Abbas is displayed on the dark brown wooden walls. The restaurant located inside this building specializes in Palestinian stuffed vegetables, and more often than not, the music that accompanies festive occasions in this place consists of pop tunes sung in Arabic rather than Spanish.

Beyond its centrality as a location for various social, cultural, and political activities, Club Palestino is a place alive, as it were, with this connection to Palestine—a place formed, negotiated, and reshaped by the intricacies of human life as it has been lived through the decades of the club's existence, always with reference to the Palestinian. In essence, Club Palestino embodies a Chilean Palestinianness and a commitment to Palestine that seem embedded within its very walls. The location of the club, its vastness, its layout, the architecture of its buildings and the design of its facilities, the pictures on the walls, the menu at the restaurant, even the marks left by shoes on its wooden floors and the stains that have merged into the fabric of chairs and rugs over the years—all these physical features seem more than just that. Rather than simply signs pointing to human practices, these features seem in and of themselves inseparable from the Palestinianness to which the place belongs, materializations of the connection to Palestine.

At the same time, Club Palestino also manifests itself as a symptom of more wide-reaching attempts to distance the Palestinian from the Chilean. That this should be the case has to do with a politics of exclusion, which in the early decades of the Palestinian presence in Chile was felt far and wide; it has to do with the neoliberal politics of (post)dictatorship and the simultaneous violence and prosperity that came with its implementation; and it has to do with the politics of continuous dispossession of Palestinians from their land. Each of these comes with a complex history, some of which I have explored in the previous chapters. In simplified terms, at Club Palestino the impact of these politics is made tangible. For those Palestinians and their descendants who experienced discrimination upon settling in Chile—an experience notably diminishing over the last few decades—the club once served as a safe haven, a place free of harassment and of being called *turcos*. As such, it served—and to some extent still serves—as somewhere for those who felt out of place to feel *in* place. Meanwhile, for the many Palestinian Chileans who experienced financial success during Pinochet's rule and have continued to do so since then, the club is a testament to that success, underlined by its grandeur and prestigious location.

Lastly, and importantly, Club Palestino constitutes in a certain sense a countermeasure to the loss of land experienced by Palestinians in the old land. In the case of Israel, as Aleida Assmann has pointed out, forgetting has meant "actively demolishing traces [of Palestine], erasing them from view and banning them from conversation" (2018, 290). In more general terms, changing the material characteristics of space, and changing how these are perceived and narrated, are two sides of the same coin. The ever-changing landscape of Palestine-cum-Israel reflects the entanglement of the material and the symbolic and continues to further blur the lines between present and absent, "real" and imagined (see Navaro-Yashin 2012). The Zionist project has not only been to carve out a physical space for the Jewish nation in Palestine, but just as much to enforce notions of belonging by symbolically inserting the presence of Israel onto the land via, for example, "Hebraizing" place names (Assmann 2018; Pappé 2006) and fashioning a historical bond with the land through archaeological practices (Abu El-Haj 2011). These practices are tightly interconnected, of course, and have worked together to substantiate and enable the enactment of Israeli claims on vast tracts of land in historical Palestine. In response, by staking claim to a piece of land and naming it *palestino*, Palestinian Chileans have, as it were, done their bit in securing a fleck on the earth's surface and reserving it for all that, to them at least, is Palestinian.

With the flags and banners out front, the centrality of concern for Palestine and the consequences of Israeli settler colonialism is solidly established at Club Palestino. From their very approach to the club, then, those who enter its physical premises are made familiar with its political premise. Far beyond the annual

Nakba commemoration ceremonies that take place at Club Palestino and else-where, politically tinted memories of Palestine inform most, if not all, of the political work being done within the club. As pointed out previously, these mem-ories do not for the most part refer to lived experience but point rather to an ongoing struggle lived by others, forming, as it were, a conglomeration of moving memories. As is especially evident within the confines of Club Palestino, Palestin-ian memory politics are spatial politics, also in diaspora.

Returns to Palestine

Club Palestino is not just a home to Palestinian cultural and social life in San-tiago. It is in myriad ways woven into the struggle for space that is at the heart of Palestinian existence a hemisphere removed from daily life in the Chilean capital. The territory that is now considered Palestine and Israel, with varying conten-tious definitions of the two, continues to play a significant role in the violence, physical and otherwise, that persistently seeps into life between the River Jordan and the Mediterranean Sea. The struggle over this land is lived not only on the ground and at the front lines, however, but also in narratives of belonging—of connection with the land itself. Among Palestinian Chileans in Santiago, accounts of travels to Palestine and (re)encounters with the places where their ancestors dwelled are often characterized by poignant descriptions of the strong emotions attached to the experience. These travels often have very direct consequences for how the connection to Palestine plays out in the Chilean context.

On a quiet afternoon I paid a visit to Fernando, who lived in a spacious apart-ment on the eastern outskirts of central Santiago with his parents and siblings. His was a lively home, full of leftovers, trinkets, and shouting between rooms. I had earlier met him at the club, where he had commandeered about a dozen of his fellow UGEP members in undertaking the painstaking task of building and decorating donation boxes made from cardboard for an upcoming campaign centered on the collection of medicine to be sent to medical facilities in Gaza. Fernando—who already seemed to have taken charge of the overall production on the club's stony terrace behind the lobby when I arrived—was painting boxes and loudly chatting with those around him with a big smile. In his early twenties, Fernando was tall and always well dressed. On later occasions he continued to strike me as involved, friendly, and constantly ending up as the center of atten-tion. Before I arrived in Santiago, Fernando had already been elected part of UGEP's leadership, and his commitment to the organization and its work was palpable. He was always present at meetings and never seemed to hesitate to take it upon himself to do the tasks no one else seemed much interested in. Besides his involvement with UGEP, he was an active *dabke* dancer and hardworking university student.

When I got to his home on that afternoon, I was promptly shown to the dining table in the kitchen where Fernando was setting up some snacks and preparing a hookah with sweet tobacco and charcoals heated up on the stove. By then I had already been greeted by everyone at home with big smiles and the customary exchange of kisses on cheeks. In the kitchen, the family's *nana* was quietly going about her work and smiled at me when I walked in. As she folded the last bits of laundry at a separate table before leaving us, Fernando and I sat down and started talking about a trip he had made to Palestine with Colegio Árabe a few years earlier. In addition to Palestine, the school trip—often referred to simply as "*la gira*" (the tour) among students—took Fernando and his classmates around several countries in the Middle East before much of the region was devastated by what was to become a long-lasting period of violence in Syria and beyond. None of what Fernando had experienced in Egypt, Syria, or Lebanon, however, could be compared to the thrill of setting foot on Palestinian soil. With the smell of the tobacco lending a fitting backdrop to our conversation, Fernando described to me how he had experienced his first encounter with Beit Jala, the hometown of his grandparents. Speaking quickly and with great enthusiasm, as was his habit, Fernando said that the most exciting part had been getting to see his grandparents' house and revisit, in very concrete terms, his family's past. It was just a matter of getting into a taxi and asking for the family house, he explained. "Beit Jala is so small that everyone knows everyone," but he still "couldn't believe it. . . . It was such a strong mix of emotions."

After his return to Santiago, Fernando had vigorously sought new ways to engage with Palestine and what he always referred to as *la causa palestina*. While visiting the place his ancestors had once called home seemed to stir in him a sense of connection with not only the place itself but with the past that bound him to it, it was not his experience of the sites of familial memory that prompted him to intensify this engagement. Rather, as he explained, he had felt invigorated and stirred into action through his encounter with the everydayness of occupation, something that had worked to solidify what he called his "full commitment to Palestine." Seeing the checkpoints and the wall lining much of the West Bank had given Fernando a corporeal understanding of the reality of occupation; but being around the people who lived under occupation's rule every day had been what really got to him: "What moves you the most is the people, how they live with occupation in spite of everything, smiling, with open arms, they keep living." To Fernando, as he traveled through Beit Jala and the West Bank, the Palestinian landscape was overflowing not only with reminders and representations of the past, but also with reminders of present struggle. As he recounted his experiences to me at the kitchen table, it became clear that his personal ties to the land via family—despite his visceral, emotional response to visiting the home of his grandparents—had somehow been diminished by the present Palestinian reality and the connection and dedication he had felt to the politics of struggle embedded in it.[1]

Once back in Santiago among friends with similar experiences, Fernando had taken a more active role within the Palestinian establishment and, among other things, become part of UGEP's core group. By the time I went to his house for a visit, he had already been back to Palestine on a trip organized by the Federation under the guise of "return," with the stated objective of familiarizing Palestinian Chileans with both the rich cultural history of Palestine and the reality on the ground in the occupied West Bank.[2] His commitment to Palestine had thus become one that was no longer confined solely to Santiago but took direct cues from his experiences elsewhere. Fernando's rhetoric on Palestine was clear, and his opinions were well-informed and coherent. Unlike many of his peers, Fernando even voiced desires to someday settle in Palestine, at least temporarily, in order to "do more for Palestine, more than I can do in Chile," and brought up concerns that the work being done within UGEP and other organizations was not "political enough." Despite identifying as right wing (*de derecha*), Fernando spoke in favor of creating stronger ties with non-Palestinian student leaders and unions often considered left wing. At the same time, like many other young Palestinian Chileans, he expressed a somewhat limited sense of connection with his Chilean surroundings. "I would go to Palestine because I don't have anything here in Chile. . . . I have my family, my friends, but nothing that I love. I don't have kids or work or a factory," he said. Fernando's own familial ties to the land might have been what brought him there in the first place, but once he was in Palestine, the experience of daily life under occupation was what cemented his devotion to the Palestinian struggle—a struggle that is never at any level separate from the land.

A Geography of Erasure

In a now classic account of Palestinian refugee camp dwellers, Sayigh ([1979] 2007) traces the development of the Palestinian people from "peasants to revolutionaries." Highlighting precisely the importance of the land and people's ties to it, Sayigh explains that while the "ex-peasant Palestinians" whom she came to know during her fieldwork were well aware that their old villages in Palestine were no longer what they used to be but had been either destroyed or become Israeli settlements, "this knowledge does not sever their ties with the land, instead it politicizes them" ([1979] 2007, 3). Importantly, as Sayigh points out, keeping the memory of the old villages alive was central to all of this. As she notes, "There is no detail of village life, from crops to quarrels, that people cannot remember in microscopic detail, in spite of—or perhaps because of—the completeness of their severance from their past" (Sayigh [1979] 2007, 2). That is, through keeping the memory of the land intact, the Palestinian camp dwellers of Sayigh's study were able to retain the link that ultimately mobilized them to become politically active (see also Davis 2011; Slyomovics 1998). As a countermeasure to both physical and symbolic erasure, then, Palestinian memories of place became countermemories.

In the case of the displaced Palestinian peasants of Sayigh's book, the land was a very tangible offset for political action and a commitment to Palestinian resistance. Despite the enormously different circumstances at play, something similar seemed to be the case for Fernando as he was spurred into action by his experience of everyday life under occupation in Palestine. Two factors link Fernando's experience with that of Sayigh's ex-peasants: memory and land, both indelibly linked to Palestine as country in the broadest sense of the word.[3] Indeed, the connection between people and the land on which they dwell—or used to dwell—is something that is often invoked in the case of Palestine, and with good reason. At least from as early on as the establishment of the state of Israel, the Palestinian story has been one of expulsion and of the subsequent fight to maintain land and, in a broader sense, presence.

The ongoing occupation of land and the construction of settlements and outposts in the West Bank beyond what many Palestinian Chileans consistently refer to as the Apartheid Wall continue to highlight that the Palestinian struggle is one for spatial presence. Indeed, the Nakba is considered a catastrophe not merely with reference to the loss of life, but further to the loss of territory and, with that, the loss of Palestinian presence on Palestinian soil (Hanafi 2012, 191). Not only has much of the old Palestinian land formally or de facto become Israeli, but with the conquering of the landscape, Israel has effected a gradual conquering of Palestinian places and thereby a gradual erasure of Palestinian existence, physical and otherwise (see Peteet 2017; Selwyn 2001). As Rebecca L. Stein (2008, 74) has pointed out, the immense changes in the geography of Palestine following 1948 marked the "most decisive" moment in a longer history of "Israeli efforts to regulate Palestinian space."[4] For the Israeli state, she further asserts, this changing geography was essential to the Zionist project, as it confined Palestinians and thus made them subject to control and, it might be added, surveillance (Stein 2008; see also Khalili 2010). As the current geography has been neatly organized around such measures, memories of what Palestine used to be have become central means of contention.

These issues came to the forefront once more in 2021 as Palestinian residents of the Sheikh Jarrah neighborhood of East Jerusalem faced imminent eviction from their homes to be replaced with Israeli settlers. Spurred by an increasing sense of urgency, videos and social media posts were spread online, with the siblings Muna and Mohammed El-Kurd taking the lead in alerting the world to the residents' reality. While this instance of efforts to displace Palestinians gained widespread attention, not least through the use of the hashtag #savesheikhjarrah, the intended removal of Palestinians from Sheikh Jarrah came about in continuation of the long-standing endeavor to ultimately—in the words of Aryeh King, the city's deputy mayor—"secure the future of Jerusalem as a Jewish capital for the Jewish people" (quoted in Khalidi 2021). In a broader sense, it revealed the settler colonial nature of the Zionist project, from 1948 to the present day, and thus served as a stark reminder of the similarities between Palestinian experiences and the experiences of indigenous populations who have faced dispossession elsewhere.

The vast majority of Palestinian Chileans have never lived under Israeli occupation, and indeed were not around when Palestine moved from Ottoman to British to Israeli hands. Whereas narratives of Palestinian resistance often circle around the notion of endurance, of staying put (see Johansson and Vinthagen 2015; Schiocchet 2013), for Palestinian Chileans, staying put under Israeli occupation was never an option because, simply, most of them had already left.[5] For them, occupying new territories—filling other spaces with a Palestinian presence—has become a way of defying erasure and loss of land elsewhere.[6] Of course, the long history of the Palestinian presence in Chile is pivotal to understanding Club Palestino as a political place within this framework. It means that most Palestinians in Chile did not live through the wave of dispossession of 1948 or the subsequent bursts of violence over the following decades until today; but according to many of the people I know in Santiago, the establishment of Palestinian places in Chile also meant that there *was* a Palestinian people before Israel, and that those who left Palestine stayed Palestinian.

In a territory where much of historical Palestine has now become Israel—and has thus effectively been erased in its previous form—memory has become an essential means of contestation. I have thus made a quick detour from Santiago to Palestine to highlight this point in particular: that the spatial dynamics of remembrance among Palestinian Chileans cannot be severed from issues of struggles for land in Palestine. The importance of Club Palestino thus surpasses its usefulness as meeting place and indeed depends on the very fact that it is a place and a piece of land that belongs, for all intents and purposes, to the distinctly Palestinian. More important, it is a place shaped to a large degree by a political premise, namely what is expressed both materially and practically as an unwavering commitment to the Palestinian cause. Its existence as a Palestinian place can therefore not be understood in separate terms from the Palestinian struggle that so many Palestinian Chileans, in various ways, consider themselves committed to. In that sense, to use Navaro-Yashin's terms, Club Palestino is constituted through a process of "making-and-believing" in which Palestine not only exists in the imagination but as a "tangibility" (2012, 6, 10). At the same time, the club is not a homogeneous and uncontested place, but one that is continuously troubled by the political context of postdictatorship and which is ultimately grounded within the uneven mnemonic landscape of Santiago.

Landscapes of Ambivalence

When I asked Andrea once how she remembered Club Palestino, she immediately started reflecting on how the landscape surrounding the club had changed in the years since she first started coming there with her family as a child. "I remember when I was little," she said laughing, "my mother had a *Citroneta*, a small Citroën. . . . We were kids, and my mom said 'Get in the car,' and we got in and she began to drive, forty kilometers per hour. . . . The Kennedy [avenue; *la Kennedy*] wasn't the same. There were no buildings. There were horses on the side of the road." The large avenue on which the club has been located since its move from central Santiago is known for a range of upscale hotels, but back then, Andrea explained, "It was strange, because we went down the Kennedy [to go to the club], and it was all an open area. There were no hotels, no Hyatt—they opened that in 1992, I think, so it's brand new. The Marriot didn't exist, the Hotel Kennedy didn't exist." Since the days when Andrea used to go to the club with her mother and brothers in their old Citroën, much has changed in Las Condes. To Andrea's memory, there was not much more to see along the Kennedy than open spaces and horses on the side of the road. In the years and decades that followed, however, Santiago has continuously expanded, with a range of constructions having sprung up around the Club Palestino compound—not least the big brand hotels that Andrea mentioned. But how does the club then fit into the urban landscape that has developed along its walls?

A few weeks after the day spent on the grass by the pool making bracelets, the time for Club Palestino's annual Gran Bazaar had arrived, and I had promised to lend a helping hand at the UGEP stand. Shortly after noon, small groups of people started setting up shop at tables lining the gravel path leading from the playground just past the entrance down toward the tennis courts. UGEP members, too, arriving with boxes full of homemade jewelry, pins, and Christmas ornaments, spread out their goods on a designated fold-out table and got comfortable on plastic chairs scattered around the path. On a day like this, the usual activities at the club had been suspended to make way for an event out of the ordinary. More and more people showed up through the gates as the sun got hotter, and as children played in the pool, extended families shared a meal from the shawarma stand, and friends strolled slowly past the Palestinian import decorations on sale while the band hired for the occasion set up their gear across the lawn at the back of the main building. Not long afterward, the music started spilling out across the pool, the grass, and the clusters of plastic tables and chairs that had been set up to accommodate the many visitors. The sound sent a jolt of energy through the otherwise tired UGEPers, and their stand was left under light attendance as most made their way toward the makeshift stage. While the band played their Arab pop tunes and the crowd clapped in appreciation, *dabke* troupes made up of young people in various formations took center stage in neatly choreographed performances of the traditional dance, their matching outfits in bright reds and greens underlining the cheerful demeanor of the smiling dancers. Although Arabic was seldom spoken at the club, numerous audience members joined in with the band, clapping and stomping their feet in the grass while singing along to the familiar lyrics.

Behind the chatter and uplifting music, however, lurked an awareness of the violence in Palestine. Months prior to Operation Protective Edge, and just about a year after 2012's Operation Pillar of Defense, there seemed to be plenty of room at the bazaar to focus on a joyous celebration of all things Palestinian. At the same time, however, the Palestinian struggle remained a subtle presence at the club on that day as on any other. At the UGEP stand, depictions of slingshots and fingers forming victory signs on smartphone covers had become the top sellers of the day, and in the basement of the main building, medicine collected for Gaza earlier was now filling up a whole room in piles of varying sizes while being organized by a group of volunteers. Even the more festive occasions at Club Palestino, then, center on an inevitably politicized connection to Palestine. During Operation Protective Edge, a big *tallarinata solidaria por Gaza*—a fancy spaghetti dinner in solidarity with Gaza—was held at the club, with all proceeds from the expensive dinner tickets going toward aid for Palestine. Even more spectacularly, the winner of the popular TV show *Arab Idol*, Mohammed Assaf—a young man who grew up in a Gazan refugee camp—gave two concerts at Club Palestino in late 2013 as part of an annual fund-raiser held by the organization Belén 2000 and with support by the Bank of Palestine. With keffiyehs and Palestinian flags being waved overhead while the excited crowd danced and sang, these concerts at the club highlighted the intricate relationship between the cultural and the political, between the lighthearted atmosphere at the club and the simultaneous and never-faltering connection with Palestine and the Palestinian struggle.[7]

All day during the Gran Bazaar, as so often happened at Club Palestino, it almost felt as if the world outside had temporarily disappeared, allowing those of us on the inside to forget that we too remained part of the cityscape around us. Only the hills and mountains on the horizon visible over the fences and gates acted as reminders that everything did not end where the club did. While Club Palestino is in many ways its own place, apart from its surroundings in both the physical and metaphorical sense, its foundation in particular political trajectories is something it shares with its surroundings. In fact, in attending to the entire cityscape of Santiago in all its discrepancies, it becomes clear that it speaks volumes on the politics that have shaped it and continue to take place within it.

Away from the younger neighborhoods in the city's northeastern parts, downtown Santiago borders on older and humbler neighborhoods. While high-rise apartment complexes continue to spring up all over the city, most of these areas are still characterized by rows of one- or two-story semidetached houses, many of which have seen better days. Oftentimes these houses have been painted in bright colors, giving the streets a festive look that does not always correspond with the general atmosphere. Small neighborhood cafés and restaurants are spread out along the streets of these districts, along with small shops and *botillerías*, liquor shops with fronts often adorned with the near omnipresent Cristal beer logo.

Scattered throughout this landscape are memorials and memory sites that recognize the many victims of dictatorship (see, e.g., Klep 2012, 2013). Among these, Villa Grimaldi, located on the eastern outskirts of the city, south of Club Palestino and Las Condes, is perhaps the best known. In 1997, the so-called Villa Grimaldi Peace Park was inaugurated on what remained of the former torture site, which had been partially demolished by the construction company that took over the property in 1987. The company had had close ties to the junta and obtained permission to raze the buildings on the site under the guise of planning to construct a residential complex (Meade 2001, 127). Shortly after the buildings had been taken down, the media became aware of what was going on and exposed the story to the public, and subsequently, following Pinochet's exit in 1990, the property was turned over to the new democratic government. It was the first of this sort of place to be transformed into a memory site in all of Latin America, and by the time of my fieldwork it had become well known (Stern 2010, 173; see also Klep 2012).[8]

Villa Grimaldi and similar places have become important parts of Santiago's geography of memory and significant venues for confronting and perhaps eventually coming to terms with the past. At the same time, these places form part of an ongoing *reckoning* with the past and reflect the fact that memory is still an issue in postdictatorship Chile (see Meade 2001, 124). Indeed, sites of memory have become important markers of an often contentious engagement with the past. Memorials that commemorate those affected by state violence can indeed "represent both an interruption and a challenge to neoliberalism's postdictatorial city" (Andermann 2015, 3), but in Santiago, this challenge appears limited to those parts of the city that seem left behind by neoliberal promises of growth and prosperity. Indeed, these memory sites, the neighborhoods in which they are placed, and the memories they harbor seem by and large forgotten in upscale districts such as Las Condes. With all its shops, coffeehouses, and restaurants, many of them part of global chains, northeastern Santiago seems to cater to a population that expects to find the same amenities here as in any other major world city. Not only does the cosmopolitanization of the area obscure its location within an otherwise unmistakably Chilean city; it also serves to hide the many layers of the past on which it has been built, from colonization to military rule and its continual influence.

Carolina Aguilera has convincingly argued that the socio-spatial segregation that appears so blatant between this new Santiago and most of the rest of the city has led to "politics of memory that are territorially discontinuous and that perpetuate forgetting in the residential environments of the country's elite" (2015, 103). In other words, within an uneven cityscape largely produced through the continued neoliberal policies introduced during the era of dictatorship, an ongoing absence of the troublesome aspects of the recent Chilean past is continuously reinforced in particular parts of the city. As Aguilera shows, the northeast of Santiago, including Las Condes, stands out as a distinct high-income area, forming a cone-like shape that expands toward the edge of the city. Tellingly, while the rest of the city is scattered with memorials dedicated to victims of state violence, this "high-income cone" is home to memorials dedicated exclusively to victims of what Aguilera terms "left-wing groups" (2015, 103). It should be noted in that regard that one of the main roads leading from the center of the city to the northeast only recently regained its pre-dictatorship name—Avenida Nueva Providencia—after having been officially known from 1980 until 2013 as Avenida 11 de Septiembre in commemoration of the day of the coup. Even with that change in mind, very different types of memories are grounded in different parts of the urban landscape.

While the connections to state violence are sometimes blurred or sought to be erased, the entire city with its uneven geography comes out of the same past and the same trajectory of political developments. The past, in other words, is "everywhere folded into the fabric of the city" (Edensor 2008, 325). The link between the current cityscape and its foundation in certain historical circumstances is not always clear, however, and many of the Palestinian Chileans whose families and businesses have grown into prosperity as a consequence of dictatorship seldom articulate this relationship. In that regard, they have in certain ways migrated away—both mnemonically and geographically—from a past toward which many retain an ambivalent attitude. This ambivalence not only has to do with the violence of dictatorship and the damage done to individuals and families whose lives were forever altered at the hands of the regime. It also is connected to the potential for rupture that lies with taking an excessively strong stance in favor of the Pinochet years and the reality that has developed from them. As was explained to me on several occasions—and became clear during UGEP meetings when issues of political affiliation were awkwardly brought up only to be quickly hushed—for both *pinochetistas* and their anti-Pinochet peers, the Chilean past holds damaging potential, threatening communal harmony and a united front for Palestine. Put simply, in the words of Laila, Palestinian Chilean organizations "don't want to pick sides." With that, postdictatorship implies varied experiences and memories of military rule, but also, for some, something of a coming together in a movement away from possibly divisive attempts to reckon with the recent Chilean past and its meaning in the present.

At the same time, no one is exempt from organizing quotidian life around the institutions that structure the everyday of postdictatorship. Both those who opposed the regime and those who profited from it now live in its afterlife. This afterlife, visible in the geography of the city, is nowhere more clearly articulated than in the socioeconomic inequality that now structures so much of life in Santiago and beyond (see Gómez-Barris 2009; Han 2012). The tall concrete buildings that make up much of the built environment in the northeastern parts of the city reflect the political climate from which they spring. Meanwhile, the older and less developed parts of Santiago seem to have been largely left behind in another time.

In the Chilean context, Club Palestino remains the main locus of a diasporic commitment to Palestine, a commitment that always takes its cue from Palestine and does not work independently of the reality there. Through commemorations and other forms of memory work, the engagement with Palestine from Santiago is temporally grounded in a present marked by a lingering past—lingering so much so, I have argued, that the mnemonic dimension of this engagement relies on an always moving form of memory rather than static recollections of a past long gone. At the same time, remembering Palestine does not take place outside the mnemonic framework put in place by the junta and those who now reject all attempts to shove its deeds and their implications under the rug. In spatial terms, as the case of Club Palestino makes evident, the Chilean and the Palestinian contexts likewise work together to set the stage for a diasporic involvement with Palestine. This involvement always implies a commitment to the land of Palestine and to the struggle for a spatial presence that continues on that land while remaining paradoxically at odds with efforts to confront and learn from the forms of repression that helped put in place the sustained neoliberal project in Chile.

Placing the Past

Despite his young age, Alex already had an aura about him of calm authority when I met him; he seemed curious about the world and spoke in a way that made it sound like he knew a lot about it already. From a family of academics, Alex was well read and serious about his studies. Likewise, he was serious about Palestine. Unlike other young Palestinian Chileans, however, he did not seem to perceive the Palestinian struggle as separate from other political issues. A few months after the Gran Bazaar at Club Palestino, I met up with Alex at the club. He had been lingering at the periphery of my social world in Santiago since the early days but had recently become more of a fixture in daily routines that centered on intensified political mobilization over the violence in Gaza during Operation Protective Edge and an equally intensified social life, the two more often than not overlapping.

It was a quiet but sunny day in August, early in the afternoon and hours before the buzz of people going to the gym, to a meeting, or to join friends for a coffee; on most weekdays the club would remain sleepy until the early evening. We settled down on a couple of wooden benches under the trees by the pool, which was left dry and unused for the winter. The day was not hot, but the sun was warm and bright, and going inside into the dark never seemed an option. As we sat there within the walls of Club Palestino, Alex drinking soda out of a plastic bottle, it was only a matter of time before the place itself came up in our conversation. Had his family always come to the club? I asked him. I already knew that his family was only Palestinian on one side, but that this side had come to play an enormous role for Alex and his siblings, who had all had very little to do with the other side after their parents' divorce.

Alex explained that "my aunts and uncles went to the club, yeah, all the young people went and everything. But I think that after the coup, during the eighties—my aunts and uncles are leftist, too—they stopped going to the club then." Although a number of factors had undoubtedly played into the decision to stay away from Club Palestino back then, it was clear that Alex saw a correlation between his family's political stance and the distance they kept to this particular place during military rule. Club Palestino, in all its relative grandeur and its direct ties to entrepreneurs who had gained financially from the dictatorship, certainly bore connotations of compliance with the Pinochet regime; and in a context where many relationships were fraying as a result of sharply drawn ideological

divides, being leftist had become irreconcilable with frequenting an establishment so thoroughly marked by conservatism and the strong links between Palestinian Chilean business owners and community leaders, on the one hand, and
the junta and its free-market objectives on the other.

"After that, in the nineties, when we, all the cousins, were little, of course we
went to the pool, like the typical 'ooh, look, there's a pool for the kids,' *cachai*?"
Alex continued. In his account of his family's relationship to the club, he framed
that relationship as interchangeably politicized and depoliticized. During the
dictatorship, his left-leaning aunts and uncles steered clear of a place that, like the
wider local and national context, was immensely impacted by political tensions.
Ultimately, the years marked by military rule prompted some, like Alex's aunts
and uncles, to avoid potential conflict while also making a political statement, as
it were, by implicitly condemning the dominant and widely repressive politics of
the era. After Pinochet's exit as head of state, however, going to the club became
a question of taking the children swimming, effectively turning it into a place of
leisure.

As the 1990s rolled around and the military regime began to loosen its grip
on all aspects of Chilean life, Club Palestino came to fully regain its position as
the hub of communal Palestinian life in all its facets. For Alex's extended family,
to which children had become an important addition, divergent politics were
tentatively pushed aside while the club became a breathing space. At the same
time, the depoliticization of the club and life within its walls had to do with
more than Pinochet's exit from the center stage of Chilean politics. With the
Israeli-Palestinian peace process and the Oslo Accords of the early to mid-1990s,
Palestinian Chileans at the club and elsewhere seemed to have much to celebrate
and enough reason to step back from overt political engagement of any kind, a
chance to enjoy a social sphere freed from political conflict, at least for a moment.
The club was never entirely free from politics, however. Not only did politics
move in tandem with wider currents in Chilean society, including an overarching
migration of Palestinian Chilean homes and institutions from the old Santiago
in Patronato to the new Santiago of the northeast; the club's very existence as a
Palestinian place made it a political place. As Alex explained,

> But really the club is more than that, it's more than the pool, *cachai*?
> It's a meeting place, a place where everyone knows you, where you have
> communal activities, because where else are you going to have them? In
> the church, fine, there are activities at church, but there's no designated
> space there for making community [*hacer comunidad*]. This place gen-
> erates identity, generates community, and for that reason, even though
> I'm not your typical *paisano* who went to Colegio Árabe and lived his

> whole adolescence here . . . I was always coming and going; but I still
> think it's important to have it and to maintain it.

To Alex, Club Palestino was the ultimate Palestinian place in Santiago. As he pointed out, there are other places dedicated to communal activities, like the churches San Jorge in Patronato and the Orthodox church in the district of Providencia between Las Condes and downtown Santiago; but although these are sometimes used for events and meetings that often have very little to do with religion, community-building is not their primary designation. With no religious overtones and little room for political ideologies, the club is both designed and continuously molded to be devoid of anything that might seem obtrusive to a cohesive, collective Palestinian realm, which is inherently political.

As Alex's account shows, however, the club is not as monolithic as it might seem at first glance. Although it remains a place of coming together, it is neither homogeneous nor free of disputes. In providing Palestinian Chileans in Santiago and beyond with a place of their own, Club Palestino also provides a place where disparate interests and attitudes unavoidably meet. To Alex's family, political developments in the Chile of the seventies and eighties meant that the club was kept at a distance until the end of dictatorship, when the children could once more be brought around to swim in the pool under more peaceful circumstances. While Club Palestino, as Alex puts it, is still the best place to "make community," it is not free of the kind of political trouble that still divides much of Chilean society along both socioeconomic and ideological lines. To a large extent, however, outside politics remain at arm's length within the club and seem to have been kept that way for most of its existence.

As described earlier, there is a sort of mindful forgetting at play within Palestinian Chilean institutions such as the club, a forgetting of troubling details of the past and uncomfortable circumstances in the present, which might cause rifts and ruptures and thus disturb the communal sphere. In many ways, Alex's reflections on Club Palestino echo this dynamic. To him and many other Palestinian Chileans, the club is a place where a sense of community is engendered, almost a kind of sanctuary for communal life. At the same time, it is a place where outside politics should be avoided, much like memories of an uncomfortable Chilean past. That the club is a place for making community means that it is a place for grand bazaars as much as for sports, coffee drinking, and committee meetings, but it also means that it is a place where Palestine and the Palestinian struggle remain present, always remembered. The finale to the week of Nakba commemorations in 2014 may have been held at Recoleta Town Hall, but formally and explicitly, as well as informally and subtly, Palestine is always remembered at Club Palestino. The past is solidly placed there, not only through the people who undertake various forms of memory work within its confines, but even through material markers of memory. From plaques to flags, rugs, and paintings to the food available in the restaurant, Palestine is kept present not only to the mind, but to the senses as well. At the same time, Club Palestino does not exist in a vacuum, but has come into its modern form within the distinct context of postdictatorship Santiago.

As an explicitly Palestinian place within the Chilean capital, Club Palestino poses a thought-provoking addition to the city's geography of memory, an addition that reflects conflicting modes of representation of the past by seemingly steering clear of this past altogether. At the same time, as pointed out above, this communal hub cannot be considered apart from the regime that in large part made the club's modern existence possible. What is interesting, then, is how Club Palestino as a Palestinian place connects yet often seems to disconnect from the Chilean past and from much of Santiago's wider mnemonic landscape. This disconnection is almost always tied to a simultaneous connection with the Palestine of both past and present. When Fernando told me the story of his trip to Palestine, he also told me the story of how he was motivated to work actively toward a free Palestine with whatever means were available to him. His narrative was not unique. In fact, many of the Palestinian Chileans I talked to about trips to Palestine stressed how being there and seeing the Palestinian reality with their own eyes had instilled in them an urgent drive to act on the injustices perpetrated against the people of Palestine and to support their struggle. While the recent Chilean past and the contentious politics that go with it have to some extent been removed from much of social Palestinian life, ultimately rendering them absent, the Palestinian past remains present, dynamic, and subject to constant representation, not least at Club Palestino.

Bordering Remembrance

Remembrance is an inherently spatial phenomenon that extends far beyond discrete sites of memory. Memory politics, in turn, are to a great extent embedded in wider geopolitical movements through which particular human and symbolic presences are variously sought to be continued or discontinued. In this chapter, I have attempted to unravel some of the knots that bind memory to space, and space to politics. By doing so, I have aimed to highlight how "we move 'through time' as much as we move 'through space'" and that the spatial and temporal are not separate spheres, but indeed both crucial to the texture of everyday life (Boyarin 1994, 21). What I have interchangeably referred to as a *movement away from* and a *mindful forgetting of* the troubling past—and to some extent the present—of Chilean politics locates dominant Palestinian Chilean memory politics alongside wider efforts at erasure and oblivion undertaken by those, often conservative, segments of Chilean society that would prefer to leave particular facets of the past dead and buried. At the same time, the forgetting—or making absent—of divisive past and present politics within the confines of Club Palestino means that the place comes to be absorbed into Santiago's mnemonic landscape despite—or perhaps rather because of—the boundaries that have been put into place around it, both literally and figuratively speaking. For many Palestinian Chileans, Palestine may be spatially removed from quotidian life but is present through practices of remembrance that are often grounded in Club Palestino. In the words of Derek Gregory (1994, 178), "the Palestinian people have consistently maintained their claims to their history, which is at the same time their geography." Certainly, for Palestinian Chileans in Santiago, history and geography are intimately linked, but in paradoxical ways.

In her book *The Architecture of Memory*, Joëlle Bahloul (1996) uses a specific house—a multifamily residence in the Algerian city of Sétif—as a constant focal point around which she lays out the interconnected histories of the Jewish and Muslim families that once dwelled there together. In Bahloul's account, the house itself appears as both an empirical and analytical entry-point into the past. Memories of family life are inextricably connected to this structure: its physical qualities, its spatial orderings, and not least the material objects that filled it and with which quotidian life once played out. One important circumstance in particular ties Bahloul's Sétif house to memory in precisely such a way, namely that the families that used to live there have since parted ways both with each other and their previously shared home. The house thus belongs to the realm of memory rather than vice versa. It is dealt with from a vantage point of both temporal and spatial distance, as a place whose particular existence as a home to these families relies on its being remembered as such. A similar mnemo-spatial relationship is evident in memories of Palestinian homes and villages occupied or destroyed in the ongoing process of Israeli encroachment onto the land of historical and present-day Palestine (Davis 2011; Khalidi 2006; Slyomovics 1998). At Santiago's Club Palestino, however, these dynamics seem to be reversed. Rather than belonging to the realm of memory, Club Palestino acts as a present-day home to a past that continuously spills over into the present and continues to be told and retold through the slowly changing physical markers of this place as much as the stories that are narrated and performed within its walls. At the same time, it is also a place for telling stories that project visions of Palestine into the future. In that sense, as Club Palestino marks the materialization of a Palestinian presence threatened elsewhere, it also echoes Gaston Bachelard's observation that "the house shelters daydreaming, the house protects the dreamer, the house allows one to dream in peace" ([1958] 2014, 28).

Club Palestino ultimately makes for a rooting down of the Palestinian in Santiago. It is a place that has been shaped and molded around Palestinian Chilean social, cultural, and political life. Like the city itself, however, Club Palestino has not gone untouched by the political rifts and ruptures that characterize the recent Chilean past. Rather, as Alex's account showed, these have shaped many experiences of the place. Deeply embedded in the broader geography of Santiago, Club Palestino is not apart from the city's mnemonic landscape. Indeed, it plays into the order of this landscape by catering to a sort of remembrance that looks across physical borders all the way to Palestine only to avert its attention from the close at hand.

On landscape and memory, Tim Ingold (1993, 152–53) writes, "To perceive the landscape is . . . to carry out an act of remembrance, and remembering is not so much a matter of calling up an internal image, stored in the mind, as of engaging perceptually with an environment that is itself pregnant with the past." This observation rings particularly true for a city like Santiago where the landscape reflects the physical, geographical changes that have come about as a result of radical politics and rapid societal developments over the last few decades. The cityscape of Santiago is indeed overflowing with the past, both in overt and subtle ways. Here the past is present in myriad ways: sometimes this presence is imposing, especially in places that have been (re)designed for engagement with the recent past and the atrocities committed during military rule; but oftentimes it poses a much more ethereal layer to the landscape. Both the obvious and the understated references to the past that can be found in the city play into a geography of memory, which, as I will return to in the following chapter, is tightly entwined with wider solidarity efforts and their limits. Ultimately, despite its walls and metal gates, it is hard to separate Club Palestino from the rest of Santiago—just as it is hard to separate the stuff of memory and politics that informs Palestinian life in this context from all the hustle and bustle of life that surrounds it.

Meanwhile, place and memory are part and parcel of a Palestinian struggle for which connections to and contestations over land are central. As I will explore in more detail in what follows, the struggle for land and for the maintenance of Palestinian places has much to do with an overall quest for Palestinian presence—a quest that informs much of Palestinian Chilean engagement with Palestine and likewise shapes mnemo-political absences. In the previous chapters we saw how interlinked practices of remembering and forgetting to a great extent inform how Palestinian Chileans relate to both past and present, and how the dynamics of memory keep them connected to a continuing history of oppression in Palestine.

At the same time, these dynamics are not unaffected by the hauntings of decades of state violence in Chile.[9] Like ghostly interventions in the landscape, both designated memorials and the subtler signs of dictatorship and its afterlife continue to make their mark, yet are often ignored within northeastern Santiago, including at Club Palestino.

"Both architecture and memory are concerned, at the outset, with the incomplete, the open, and the relational," writes Bishop (2014, 557). Even as it creates borders and reinforces wider political tugs-of-war between remembrance and oblivion, Club Palestino, like all other places, remains in flux, subject to potential transformations that might take it beyond what it was intended to be. And as an only pseudo-fixed point in the mnemonic landscape of the city, its relation to the past depends entirely on how it is constituted in the present. However, as a distinct *bundle* within the mnemonic landscape of the city, Club Palestino simultaneously marks an abandonment of Chilean memory while effectively marking a continuation of the memory politics evident in the geography of the city. It allows disruptive reminders of (post)dictatorship to be left still and unmoving at the gates while moving memories of Palestine are constantly kept present. In broad terms, then, Club Palestino is illuminating of the ways in which memories may travel across vast distances and at the same time be faced with boundaries created locally. In the city, various pasts overlap and clash with one another along fault lines that are impressed in the landscape and create dents and barriers that run along the edges of dissonant and irreconcilable bundles of memories. What happens when these bundles—or bubbles—come undone and burst into a multifaceted public space will be explored in the following chapter.

SEEING AND BELIEVING

In July 2014, disaster struck in Gaza.[1] The response in Santiago to the crisis of Operation Protective Edge was immediate and, so it seemed at the time, almost all-encompassing, as if a filter had been drawn over usual quotidian activities and all excess energy was put toward manifesting outrage at what was taking place in Palestine. UGEP quickly mobilized all its forces to respond to the violence with protest. Along with other organizations, the core group set up a number of protests and demonstrations, informative events, and campaigns. Of the public interventions that took place during this time, a handful of widely publicized protest marches were by far the best attended and most spectacular, and they will be the main focus here. However, several other types of demonstrations were carried out in the wake of Operation Protective Edge, including a candlelight vigil and a *pintatón* ("paintathon"), a public painting of cars with pro-Palestine slogans that took place simultaneously in several Chilean cities. The leadership of UGEP also decided to go through with a conference joining old members and interested newcomers from around the country in discussing the future of the organization as well as debating the way forward for *la causa* in Chile. The conference had already been planned before the Israeli incursion into Gaza but seemed only more important because of it. Further, inspired by the New York chapter of Students for Justice in Palestine, UGEP instigated a campaign during which thousands of fake letters of arrest were distributed to households all over Santiago to call attention to the many Palestinian prisoners who were held without charges by Israeli authorities.

Despite the apparent disenchantment with establishment politics among many Chileans, the country has a very strong tradition of popular protest at both ends of the political spectrum (see, e.g., Power 2002, 2004). Since the resurrection of the Chilean student movement in 2011 during the so-called Chilean Winter, student protests had once again become a fixture in the city center during my time in Santiago, and public demonstrations of all kinds had become a common sight in the city (see Frens-String 2013; Guzman-Concha 2012; Villalobos-Ruminott 2012). Although perhaps not as intense as the protests and consequent clashes with police that took place in 2011,[2] these demonstrations certainly made an impression on their surroundings. While engagement with the political establishment might have weakened in the wake of military rule, ongoing events of popular mobilization point to a kind of political imagination that asks what can be done beyond the confines of government and state institutions (see Hayden 2014). This was indeed the case during the course of Operation Protective Edge.

In previous chapters I have looked at how Palestinian Chileans relate to both Palestine and the Israeli settler colonial project in postdictatorship Santiago through oftentimes highly spatialized negotiation of moving memory and its boundaries in daily life. The public demonstrations that served to make noise during the Israeli attacks on Gaza were, in that sense, but the latest among longstanding efforts to remember Palestine within the Santiago cityscape, some of which, like Club Palestino, had already materialized and settled into the landscape. I take these events as the starting point for an exploration of the (un)confinability of memory as a phenomenon that both moves and is moved by people. The protests that took place in the wake of Operation Protective Edge lend interesting perspectives to the dynamics of moving memory not least because they themselves were born of movement—in both literal and figurative terms—from the confines of the Palestinian establishment and Club Palestino and out into the open spaces of the city. With that in mind, this chapter is about what happens when memory moves to the street.

"Our house walls enable us to forget the outside even when it is being experienced as unbearable," writes Ariella Azoulay (2013, 200). While Club Palestino might be a house—a whole compound, rather—that facilitates both remembrance and forgetting, the boundaries it creates in the mnemonic landscape can never shield its dwellers entirely from what surrounds them, nor do those dwellers, as we saw in chapter 3, ever manage to completely shield themselves. In this chapter I move beyond more fixed points in the mnemonic landscape and begin to scrutinize how remembrance and its politics are negotiated in public spaces that are malleable and susceptible to everyday human intervention while harboring contentious traces of the past. The considerations put forth in this chapter do not limit themselves to the realm of public protest, however. Rather, they are to a great extent informed by what happened between demonstrations. In that regard, I look to the use of social media, and particularly to the sharing of images, to approach an understanding of the importance of visibility and presence for the politics at play. On platforms such as Facebook and Instagram, harrowing images from Gaza were widely shared during the 2014 incursion, often alongside messages of outrage and support for the victims. This chapter, then, is also about the relationship between images, on the one hand, and visibility on the other.

The bundles of memories that constitute mnemonic landscapes can sometimes clash and challenge each other, making the landscape as such inherently contentious as people produce silences as they make noise and create absences by making visible and enforcing the presence of particular pasts rather than others. In that sense, opening up the mnemonic landscape to memories of an elsewhere also entails the possibility of closing it off to others. Meanwhile, in a broader sense, closures and openings in the mnemonic landscape of the city never exist entirely apart from one another. Indeed, they often seem to rely on each other to create and challenge the boundaries that serve to protect mnemo-political projects but that often prove unstable and easily penetrable. Starting from an interrogation of how memory moves, or fails to do so, in such a feebly divided public space, I aim to shed further light on what has been called "the Janus-like effort entailed in looking back to the past and forward to the future at the same time" (Hirsch and Miller 2011, xii). The protests and demonstrations that took place in Santiago during the Chilean winter of 2014 did just that: they looked back and looked ahead at the same time, tying in not only with a history of popular dissent in the Chilean capital but also with the Palestinian struggle itself.

To the Street

On a sunny and mild Sunday afternoon in early August, the regular Palestino football match at the stadium at La Cisterna was followed by a march for Gaza, the latter organized specifically so that the two would not coincide. Like many other match-goers that day, a small group of us headed straight from the stadium toward downtown Santiago and the protest following the game. Weaving smoothly through traffic and through the city in Andrés's little red car, we made it from La Cisterna to the outskirts of Patronato, from where we could easily walk to the march. Andrés was in his late thirties and stood out among his friends with his sharp political insights and vast historical knowledge. Well past his student days, Andrés worked a steady job in the city but still made it a priority to take part in Palestine-related activities and could be found on the bleachers at La Cisterna for most Palestino games. Older and both better read and more widely traveled than most of the Palestinian Chileans I had spent time with in UGEP and elsewhere, Andrés approached most issues with calm and measured skepticism but nonetheless made a point of doing what he felt he could for Palestine and the Palestinian cause. He was no stranger to protest marches and had likewise been a leading force behind several initiatives associated with both well-established and more short-lived Palestinian organizations.

Andrés parked the car in one of Patronato's quieter pockets, a few blocks from the San Jorge church where the procession was to start out. We walked down toward the church, accompanied by dust and stray dogs, and got there about ten minutes after the march was set to start. In other words, our timing was perfect. Within minutes the narrow street in the heart of Patronato was full of people softly shifting on their feet, waiting for their cue to start walking. Everywhere were familiar faces. By sheer coincidence we found ourselves right next to Tarek and a handful of his fellow UGEP members. Three of them were standing around holding a large piece of cloth made to look like a keffiyeh, waiting for the march to kick off. Then, out of the blue, Fernando came around with a bottle of red paint and offered us some for our hands; it was meant to look like blood. The UGEP group quickly put down their massive keffiyeh, briefly leaving it on the ground in order to have their hands washed over with paint, the red turning pale pink as it dried on their skin. Slowly, the large group of people that was crammed together on that narrow street began to move. Palestinian flags, balloons, and banners were raised up against the blue sky, and the chants built in volume as we made our way further downtown: "¡A romper, a romper relación con Israel!" (Break, break relations with Israel!).

Operation Protective Edge had resulted in a tangible shift in gear within and beyond the Palestinian sphere. While the onslaught went on, demonstrations were carried out more than once a week, each growing in size as the Israeli incursion failed to come to a hasty conclusion. These demonstrations were not only attended by Palestinian Chileans and those connected with the Palestinian establishment. As with most public events that were framed as being pro-Palestine, indigenous Mapuche groups were represented at every march during this crisis, as was the Communist Party. At the biggest of these marches along the avenue of La Alameda, protesters were likewise joined by supporters of Chile's most popular football team, Colo-Colo, as they walked along with their own banners calling for peace and singing their own fight songs. Moreover, a number of organizations and political parties besides the Communists were represented among the Santiaguinos of all ages and backgrounds who had come together to show their discontent with the situation and to call for the Chilean government to take diplomatic measures to put a stop to the crisis.

As protesters took over various public spaces in the city for limited periods of time during Operation Protective Edge, they reconfigured those spaces with their presence in the process. Yet the political actions that came to the fore during the Israeli incursion into Gaza in mid-2014 were not only spatially oriented. Rather, they were configured along a particular temporal axis whose categories of past, present, and future were not necessarily linear and straightforward, a configuration that reflected both Chilean and Palestinian contexts. The mobilizations around this particular cause that took place during my time in Santiago did not stand apart from wider mobilizations, nor did they attract a homogeneous group of Palestinian Chileans. Although many of the political demonstrations for Palestine around this time had been organized by groups connected with the Palestinian establishment, this was not exclusively the case. Indeed, the fact that Palestinian institutions like UGEP and the Federation had been bypassed by outsiders on several occasions irked members of these organizations who were concerned about having their own role diminished and the Palestinian cause somehow diluted with the influx of various interests. Yet placing these demonstrations within public space meant that a broad range of protesters inevitably turned up and took part.

Following the first of the marches for Gaza that took place during this particular spate of violence, several speakers had lined up next to each other on the steps of the old colonial-style building downtown where the relatively short procession had concluded. Having set off from a small pedestrian shopping street close to the presidential palace at La Moneda, the march had gone only a couple of blocks before it came to a standstill, reportedly because only a confined demonstration rather than an actual march had been permitted by the authorities. Thus, crammed along the street that ran between La Alameda and the central Plaza de Armas, protesters with flags, banners, and a large number of black balloons had come to a halt in front of the building. Their chants quickly faded out as the day's announced speakers took over, circulating a blue-and-white megaphone between them. Besides Tarek, who had spoken briefly on behalf of UGEP, the speakers included representatives of various organizations, and not only Palestinian Chilean. As Tarek himself would later lament during our lunch with Laila, both Communist and Mapuche speakers had also made their way up the steps of the building and reached for the megaphone. Stressing solidarity, these speakers had highlighted the commonalities between their own work and the Palestinian cause. While a Communist Party spokesperson explicitly stated that "the only way forward is solidarity," a Mapuche speaker talked at length about the intersections between his own and the Palestinian struggle and concluded his speech by stating that "it's all the same struggle, a struggle for land."

The connections thus forged between Palestinian Chilean politics and wider struggles within Chilean society were often met with dismay and uneasiness. As described in chapter 3, members of the core group of UGEP were concerned that the presence of the Mapuche and representatives of the Communist Party at demonstrations would take away the focus from Gaza and thus, in effect, hijack them. Fernando was also skeptical of outsider participation, especially by Communist and Mapuche groups, at rallies in support of Palestine. During Operation Protective Edge, he clarified his position to me during a conversation: "At the marches you always see the Communists. . . . The Communists are with us because they're all about justice, human rights, and all that. I think that's why. Also the Mapuche. . . . But I don't like that the Communist Party shows up and uses our march as a platform for their own cause. Sure, come with your banners and everything, but don't take advantage." Nevertheless, he added, "it's more support and a part of the population that we [UGEP] don't usually reach." Fernando was clearly ambivalent with regard to the presence of these perceived outsiders but echoed the many voices bemoaning the fact that UGEP, the Federation, and the Palestinian establishment as such had to share their platform. At the same time, the reluctance to engage in solidarity efforts between these institutions and other political formations cannot be solely explained by concern for the limelight. Rather, I suggest, it ties in with an overall reluctance to engage with the beyond-personal as well as with related attempts at mnemonic bordering that serve to safeguard certain presences rather than others. In this particular case, an unease related to postdictatorship as well as local postcolonial politics had become situated in the public space of the city and expressed with direct reference to the confrontations this public space facilitated.

During our long conversation at Club Palestino around the time of Operation Protective Edge, Alex and I also got to talking about politics and protest. I was especially curious about his perspective on popular mobilization because I knew him to have been politically active both within and beyond organizations like UGEP. Despite having gone to a private school, Alex was one among only a few people I got to know in Santiago to speak of having taken part in the Chilean student movement. As he explained to me on this day at the club, Chile became "paralyzed" when the so-called Penguin Revolution[3] took off in 2006 (see Frens-String 2013; Guzman-Concha 2012). In his mid-twenties when I met him, Alex had "lived just one month of dictatorship" and was thus part of an age group where "we were all born and raised in democracy," without fear of repression. So, although it did not make sense to Alex and his schoolmates to occupy their own private school, he explained, they had not hesitated to attend protest marches and had even helped public school students who were undertaking occupations and strikes by bringing them food. When I asked Alex if this was all a display of solidarity then, he told me, "Yes, but I understood that it was everyone's issue, *cachai*? It wasn't their struggle; it was everyone's struggle [No era su lucha; era la lucha de todos]."

Although Alex might have considered the politics of the student movement relevant as part of "everyone's struggle," other young Palestinian Chileans did not share his perspective. As a prominent member of the UGEP leadership during subsequent student uprisings, Alex explained that his involvement in the student movement had stayed a separate matter: "UGEP had conflicting opinions on the demands of the students and the possible solutions . . . so in the end we never managed to agree on a position, to compromise." In Alex's understanding of the issue, the fact that UGEP ultimately decided to stay out of the student movement had much to do with the more overtly leftist, even communist, politics of UGEP itself in the 1980s—a legacy that the new leadership had sought to put behind them in order to position the organization as more ideologically neutral. Rather than get directly involved with national politics since then, Alex added, the focus of UGEP and other organizations was to "generate debate" rather than take a singular stance.[4] This ideal of neutrality seemed tightly connected with wider negative perceptions of particularly leftist social movements within Chilean society. As was pointed out to me by several people, the era of postdictatorship was one in which the political fault lines between left and right—*la izquierda* and *la derecha*—had been drawn so rigidly that prejudice and animosity made it difficult to look beyond differences. Especially leftist movements and their traditional modes of dissent carried what Fernando would later describe to me as "stigma."

What Alex described with regard to the student movement rang true for any other struggle or cause that could potentially spur efforts at solidarity from within the Palestinian establishment; any overt connection would most likely be rejected or avoided to the extent possible. The rejection of acts of overt solidarity did not necessarily always indicate a lack of sympathy but seemed rather to go hand in hand with a general unwillingness to bring any non-Palestine-related politics into the communal realm. As we saw with Tarek in chapter 2, however, some people simply felt entirely unmoved to get involved in any issue that did not directly affect them. Whether dealt with in affective or more practical terms, rejection of this kind effectively plays into wider attempts to silence or make invisible irritating pasts, thereby also occluding their connection to present realities. In turn, these attempts pivot around a desire for boundaries that leave certain pasts still, stagnant, and unmoving, effectively rendering them absent. In that regard, public space and its potential for confrontation play a particular role.

Picturing the Present

While protests and other public demonstrations took place several times a week during Operation Protective Edge, social media sites, especially Facebook and

Twitter, were buzzing nonstop with images of human and material destruction, news from Gaza, and outbursts of anger and frustration. Some photographs being shared showed small children in hospital beds, heads wrapped in bandages, skin marked by shrapnel. Others portrayed crying women and desperate-looking men carrying the injured out of the rubble. A particularly horrific series of images—and one that was widely reproduced, not only on social media—showed four boys running on the beach in Gaza and the subsequent cloud of dust from the aerial shelling that left them all dead.[5] Besides these images and more, videos showed bombardments of the densely populated Gaza Strip from a distance, a gray mass of debris reaching into the air after each blast.

With these images, both still and moving, destruction and violence in Gaza became something that was witnessed daily, albeit from a great distance, by Palestinian Chileans and their online networks. Some, however, chose to focus on resistance rather than destruction. An active user of social media, Fernando took to circulating a mix of captioned images and links to articles during the incursion into Gaza. Rather than photographs of injured bodies and rubble, Fernando's feed featured mostly pictures of stone-throwing Palestinians among political cartoons damning the Israeli violence, as well as brief comments accompanied by links offering further reading. Fernando likewise shared photos from the demonstrations that took place in Santiago in support of Gaza, but for the most part his posts focused on events in Palestine and included Twitter reports with updates on rising casualty numbers, along with the more hopeful imagery of resistance.

The internet, and especially social media, came to play a significant role in the mobilization efforts that followed the outbreak of violence on a massive scale in Palestine. The wide circulation of images from Gaza had very real effects not only in Santiago, of course. As pointed out by Mark R. Westmoreland and Diana K. Allan (2016, 206), "images of Israel's devastating 2014 invasion of Gaza made starkly visible—in ways that text could not—the extreme disparity between the two sides and the excessive, overbearing military might of Israel, galvanizing unprecedented international solidarity with Palestinians in the Occupied Territories." Perhaps to an even greater extent than ever before, violence was directly broadcast on social media during Operation Protective Edge as shared photographs evoked an ongoing, painful military incursion (see Naguib 2008, 243; see also Axel 2004). The images were shared widely and seemed to have an immense impact on those who were doing the sharing. If anything, the constant outpouring of violent imagery along with brief texts professing frustration and calling for action made the connection between Chile and Palestine, in particular Gaza, tangible. Simply put, it provoked a sense of urgency in highlighting the simultaneity of fear, attacks, and threats of imminent destruction.

"Being a spectator of calamities taking place in another country is a quintessential modern experience, the cumulative offering by more than a century and a half's worth of those professional, specialized tourists known as journalists. Wars are now also living room sights and sounds," wrote Susan Sontag (2003, 16). At play in the case of the relation of Palestinian Chileans to violent imagery from Gaza, however, is more than a "quintessential modern experience." Rather, it is perhaps a quintessential Palestinian experience, whereby those who feel connected to the Palestinian struggle share in the frustration of their fellow spectators and are mobilized into action against what they witness. During Operation Protective Edge, at least, brutal images were very much "presented as an impetus to action" and thus worked through the assumption that "vision contains a compelling potential" (Allen 2009, 169–70).[6] Importantly, there was an affective quality to the images being shared. Visual reminders of present Palestinian realities led to a stirring up of emotions among people, underscoring that "*seeing* leads not only to knowledge but also, importantly, to *feeling*" (Murphy 2019, 6; italics in the original). Quite simply, the images were moving. At the same time, they relied on a mnemonic grounding to garner the response they received among people like Fernando. It was an awareness—rational and affective—of the temporal continuity of violence in Palestine that allowed these images to resonate and to work as powerfully as they did. In Fernando's case, personal memories of Palestine undoubtedly intensified this resonance, but many others who had never set foot on Palestinian soil shared responses similar to his. To them, witnessing the events of the present through the prism of shared understandings of the past implied that Palestine was present and stayed with them, throughout this period and for long after.

The temporally and spatially outstretched nature of colonial violence became evident in this instance, with memories of a past lived elsewhere surging into the present in the city. In that sense, I continue to argue, memory moves in the double sense of the word: it stirs something in people as it travels within and between both temporal and spatial domains, not least through images and other media. However, the attentiveness to violence and its implications did not translate easily for some into the Chilean context, where communists and Mapuche remained unwelcome presences. Connerton (1989, 2) asserts that "we experience our present world . . . with reference to events and objects which we are not experiencing when we are experiencing the present." To that I might add that, at least in this case, the present is experienced with reference to events and objects not experienced *where* the present is experienced. When images and stories are shared on social media in real time, such as they were during Operation Protective Edge, memories pertaining to an unfinished past effectively travel across spatial boundaries and bring about a shift in how people perceive of and act within the here and now.[7]

. For Palestinian Chileans who know very well the long history of Palestinian struggle and look back to the Nakba as a watershed moment—not only for the Palestinian people as a whole but for the politicization of their own Palestinianness—engaging with this sort of moving memory binds them to the continuously unfolding reality in Palestine. Despite the prevalence of social media and their unmistakable importance for political mobilization, however, the space of the city remained crucial to protests against the violence in Gaza. Indeed, as much as the role of the digital deserves attention in cases such as this one, popular politics and dissent still hinge on the existence and use of public space (see Parkinson 2012; Tawil-Souri 2012; see also Tawil-Souri and Aouragh 2014).[8] Social media provided important platforms for expression, communication, and sharing during the onslaught in 2014, but it was Palestinian Chileans taking to the streets of Santiago with their protests that made for the most exceptional display of their connection to a reality otherwise far removed from their daily lives.

Making Noise

Beyond what happens behind closed doors among government officials, politics easily becomes a matter of being heard and seen. All political demonstrations I attended or witnessed in Santiago relied on voices and instruments to make themselves heard. Rhythmic chants were often flanked by tunes played by small marching bands, a variety of drums and horns creating sounds not easily matched—in volume nor musicality—by chanting human voices. At the same time, the visual played an enormous role. Besides banners, flags, and cardboard signs, protesters often included their own bodies in the visualization of their message, wearing particular clothes or using face and body paint to bring striking color to their procession. Together, these forms of creating visibility and making noise have, in effect, come to form a certain repertoire, "a limited set of routines that are learned, shared, and acted out" and that have emerged "from struggle" (Tilly 1995, 41–42). This repertoire of protest has developed within a context largely marked by unrest caused by social inequality and the disparate lived realities within the Chilean population, but it is also closely linked to the despondency at play when it comes to establishment politics, as it goes directly against the orderly, quiet politics practiced in meeting rooms and halls by people in suits.

While making noise is a common strategy that implies both producing actual noise and establishing ways of gaining continued attention, the role of seeing and being seen adds a certain level of complexity to the issue of political presence.

The last demonstration I attended before leaving Santiago was a protest march that took up all of La Alameda, going from Plaza Italia to La Moneda and joining thousands of angered Santiaguinos to call for an end to the violence in Gaza. From the underground metro station in the center of Plaza Italia, the crowd was audible before it became visible. Flowing down the busy stairs to the large station were chants and chatter, scattered drumbeats, and the noise of thousands of shuffling feet. Aboveground, with the gathering within range of vision, the sight of the many protesters only seemed to intensify the abundance of sounds filling the plaza as the march was about to take off.

This march would become the largest of its kind and one of the most talked-about pro-Palestine events in Santiago during the 2014 incursion into Gaza. On the day of the protest, Operation Protective Edge had already been going on for several weeks, and it seemed evident that more and more people had become aware in that time of the atrocities being committed. Moreover, this was the first of the marches for Gaza to go down La Alameda, perhaps one of the most symbolically charged roads in the Chilean capital. Although protests of all sorts were never confined to downtown Santiago, this central avenue, leading from a traffic hub in the center of the city way out to its western parts, seemed the go-to place for large marches. As one of the city's main thoroughfares, La Alameda offers protesters a real possibility of shutting down traffic and disrupting the usual flow of the city. Its trajectory from Plaza Italia down past La Moneda locates La Alameda at the very center of the city, allowing marchers to move from one of the city's most popular meeting places to the very seat of political power. On this march down the avenue, as the sun lent a bit of heat to the otherwise cool winter air, protesters effectively made themselves seen and heard within Santiago's most notable public place.

At this march in particular, a large variety of means were employed to create a spectacular array of sights and sounds. Besides a huge number of home-made signs—often simply pieces of cardboard fastened to some kind of stick and painted with catchphrases and basic symbols—protests featured impressive amounts of balloons, large, professionally crafted banners, and Palestinian flags in great numbers. Joining these material means of visual communication was a specially made protest piece: an expanse of heavy cloth depicting the Palestinian flag, so large that it had to be carried by dozens of protesters who struggled to keep it off the ground as they held it stretched out over the pavement. Adding to this was a range of sounds and noises augmenting the spectacle of protest. Along the formation of people, chants spread out in waves of sound from several epicenters along the procession: "¡No más muertes de niños inocentes! ¡Palestina vencerá, el sionismo caerá!" (No more deaths of innocent children! Palestine will overcome, Zionism will fall!). As soon as one chant died out, someone in the crowd was quick to lead the way with another. The simple messages, along with the strength of these chants, made them travel quickly along the train of people marching; few protesters who had turned up in support of Gaza could possibly disagree with what was shouted out, and the choice of uncomplicated words and the simple staccato of the chants meant that everyone could take part. Indeed, at times it sounded like everyone did.

These chants were not alone in creating a multilayered soundscape that moved along La Alameda and even traveled beyond: football fans were singing their battle songs, and people were shouting into megaphones. The most imposing sounds, however, were those made by bands of musicians who had brought along a variety of drums and horns that easily overpowered human voices as the band members playfully danced their way through the procession. Some of these musicians were parts of larger groups of performers that included dancers in more or less festive attire; others seemed to have simply come to make noise. Together, the jumble of sounds created by voices and other instruments made for a fantastical, echoing soundscape. Although focused by and large on Palestine and the situation in Gaza, both the visual and auditory elements of the demonstration drew on the same repertoire of protest, sharing similarities with forms of protest prevalent in large parts of the world, here developed in unison with the changing politics of late twentieth and early twenty-first-century Chile.

During a conversation with Fernando about the ongoing campaigns and demonstrations in mid-2014, I pointed out that people and groups associated with *la izquierda* were disproportionately represented at protests. In response, Fernando alluded to the conflict-ridden past of protest marches as a popular form of contention, but quickly glossed it over: "There's a stigma with the marches, but that's just one way of demonstrating [*manifestarse*]. If you don't like marches, we have other activities [that you can take part in]." The stigma that Fernando referred to meant that especially conservative actors were few and far between at the marches for Gaza. That stigma, however, had not deterred people like Fernando and Tarek from engaging in precisely such a repertoire of protest.

In present-day Santiago, marches and demonstrations have become parts of a popular political practice that regularly brings the spectacular theatricality of protest into the realm of daily life. At many of these events, memory has retained a central position, as the marches and demonstrations inscribe "in the cityscape the ongoing impact of dictatorial terror" (Andermann 2015, 5). Even for protesters whose cause does not carry an explicit reference to the era of dictatorship or the further-reaching Chilean condition of postcoloniality—the Palestinian, to mention one—the modes of protest employed carry resemblances to past expressions of dissent and thus cannot be separated from the development of these forms into an ever-relevant repertoire of protest. This development has relied on changing political atmospheres, not least during the latter half of the twentieth century. Popular protest is thus to a great extent temporally oriented, whether those taking part are aware of it or not; political demonstrations in public space look to both past and future.

Protest, Place, and Visibility

Of course, the many marches that fill the public spaces of the city do not represent the only way in which space is occupied and politicized. In chapter 4 I looked at the position of Club Palestino within what I call Santiago's mnemonic landscape and explored the politics that have gone into spatial developments in the city over the years. The particular dynamic between protest and place, however, holds a potential distinct from that of other spatially expressed politics. Indeed, protests and demonstrations on streets and squares work to transform a public, shared space into a politically charged space where people can express themselves and, in turn, call for response (see Kaplan 2004, 11; McFarlane 2011). Although those in power, those perhaps at whom protest is aimed, do not always respond to such protest, others often do. Whether a public demonstration prompts an onlooker to join in—or perhaps stage an impromptu and singular counterprotest—there is movement and dialogue. Moreover, the location of protest within public space highlights the connection between presence, or presentness, and visibility (Hénaff and Strong 2001, 6). Out in the open, protests are seen—indeed witnessed—by a range of onlookers and, as described above, likewise most often heard and otherwise sensed.

During Operation Protective Edge, social media came to play an enormously important part in rendering both visible (via images and text) and audible (via video) the destruction in Gaza, prompting responses that were not necessarily confined to the virtual realm. Lina Khatib (2012, 1) has claimed that political struggle "is an inherently visually productive process. It is also itself visual to a large degree: It is a struggle over presence, over visibility." The response to Operation Protective Edge from within the Palestinian establishment in Santiago showed just that; promptly, Palestinian Chileans took to social media to share reports from Gaza and express their indignation at the ongoing bursts of violence, and almost just as quickly, they took to planning and carrying out protests and other activities designed to make visible and present the Palestinian struggle. Meanwhile, while hearing and being heard seem relatively straightforward as means of gaining influence, sight and visibility appear as double-edged swords that facilitate both violence and resistance to it.

The marches for Gaza that took place in mid-2014 were indisputably spectacular; with the magnitude of people, sounds, and visuals at these demonstrations,
they took over significant stretches of public space and became inescapable to
everyone in their general vicinity. As a result, they made for an imposing presence
of the Palestinian struggle within the Santiago cityscape, based to a great extent
on the sheer visibility (and audibility) of the events themselves. By thus calling
attention to the Palestinian cause, the protesters in effect "re-presented" it, causing it to reappear within a Chilean context where it remains absent from the public sphere most of the time (Connerton 1989, 69; with reference to Lévy-Bruhl
1935; see also Gregory 1994, 104). The presence that was established on these
occasions had much to do with the events' form, and in particular the spectacular
theatricality that to a great extent characterized them (see Bayat 2003; Sjørslev
2012). If "so much of politics is now about that which can and must be 'seen,'
about 'spectacle'" (Khalili 2010, 125), then the marches for Gaza definitely put
Palestine into the Chilean political arena, making use of a "space of appearance"
within which they could be seen (Springer 2010; with reference to Arendt 1958).

At the same time, this spectacular presence was bound to "the prohibition
upon seeing, the effort to make 'unseen'" as "the necessary double of spectacular politics" (Khalili 2010; see also Swedenburg 2003). Such efforts at absenting
rather than presenting have been central to the Israeli nation-state project where
both Palestinian histories and Palestinian places are subject to potential erasure
and are likewise at play in relation to mnemonic boundary-making in Santiago
and elsewhere. As Gil Z. Hochberg (2015, 3) rightly points out, "the oft-quoted
Zionist phrase 'a land without a people for a people without a land' encapsulates
a profound failure or refusal to see, and thus to recognize the political agency
of, the native Palestinian inhabitants."[9] Likewise, as Sari Hanafi (2012, 190) con-
tends, a certain "institutionalized invisibility of the Palestinian people both feeds
and is being fed by Israel's everyday settler-colonial practices," which, he asserts,
go hand in hand with what he calls the "spacio-cidal" Israeli project.[10]

Club Palestino can be understood within this wider framework as a territory
claimed as Palestinian, gaining much of its political (and social) meaning from
the fact that space is so contested in the old land. Similarly, marches and demonstrations can be seen as claims on an ever-negotiated public space, if only for a
limited time: blocking traffic, possessing that space, and making a cause visible,
audible, and indeed present. Although both involve the overt politicization of
space, then, popular protests like the marches for Gaza foreground spectacular presences that both challenge the bordering of politics in the landscape and
seek to create new boundaries between what is considered worth remembering
and what should rather have been left forgotten. Especially a shared Palestinian

past—albeit for the most part not lived—remains a central social force in this context, and no doubt adds fuel to the will for a Palestinian presence in Santiago and Chile.

By drawing on a repertoire of protest and placing their demonstrations at the epicenter of Chilean politics, past and present, those who marched for Gaza during Operation Protective Edge did so within a distinct historical context. They were located within something of a double-edged "historical time," emplaced within two distinct sets of "historical narrative of political action that looks back to the past . . . and forwards to an imagined set of possibilities for the future" (Lazar 2014, 91; see also Koselleck 2004). For Palestinian Chileans, the quest for ongoing presence is not only temporally oriented but has great bearing on practices and understandings that rely on and indeed focus on space. The Palestinian struggle for presence, in that sense, is one that transcends boundaries of time and space; it is both here and there, then and now. Because of the threat to both spatial and temporal presence—bodies and materials present on the land as well as a shared past remembered—posed by Israel and the Zionist project, the response for Palestinians must inevitably be to fight for that presence.[11]

Maintaining presence requires the negotiation of outside reminders that refuse to stay occluded from view, however. Although Fernando, Tarek, and others expressed irritation at the presence of communists and Mapuche representatives at the marches for Gaza, Laila was quicker to point out the potential in gathering a diverse crowd:

> In reality no one mixes with the Chileans [*los chilenos*]. . . . It's like they look at them the same way they looked at us [Palestinian Chileans] when we first came here. But that kind of thing has to stop. The guy [who organized the first march for Gaza during Operation Protective Edge] got involved with the FECH [the Student Federation of the University of Chile], all the students, and he put together a march with thirty thousand people, *cachai*? Even though he's very communist and always focused on everything communist . . . , ultimately it didn't bother him calling on the FECH, calling on the people of *la derecha* and anyone that wanted to join. And what did he achieve? An enormous march— enormous, enormous. And I feel that what happened within UGEP was [complaining that] it was full of communists, it was full of the Mapuche, it was full of people from the university, it was full of who knows what else. . . . When they talked [at the march] they didn't talk about Palestine one hundred percent, they talked about their own political interests, and that's fine; but at least those people showed up, and they're

the ones that support us, *cachai*? . . . It shouldn't matter who shows up. What does it matter who shows up? The message of that march was clear: We want a free Gaza. If a thousand communists showed up, it doesn't matter. Gaza is the message. That's the message.

The potential that Laila saw in bringing a wide array of people together in marching for Palestine was not necessarily recognized as such by many others I spoke with. At the same time, her comments highlight that no matter what her fellow UGEPers and others might believe, the politics of their Chilean surroundings cannot be fully escaped, especially not during public demonstrations.

The spatial aspects of presence, I argue, are pivotal to understanding the potential in public protests. As was dealt with in more depth in chapter 4, space, land, and territory have been intrinsic to the Israeli colonial project since its earliest days. Meanwhile, the current conditions of life for Palestinians in the West Bank and Gaza are by all means expressions of efforts to control and manipulate the geography of these disputed territories; walls, checkpoints, and practically all aspects of local infrastructure reflect dominance and simultaneously reveal how Israel uses the landscape as a real-world laboratory within which the state is able to test the technologies that sustain its position as a major power (see Bowman 2004; Gould 2014a, 2014b; Graeber 2015; Halper 2015; Peteet 2005; Selwyn 2001). Through domination of the landscape, Israel by and large dominates the very basis for Palestinian life. At the same time, this domination implies a suppression of local place-making, as Palestinians to a great extent are hindered from building, as it were, a world of their own (see Tawil-Souri 2012, 90). As much as space is vulnerable to power and can be made into a vehicle for oppression, however, it is likewise a foundation for contention, for resistance. In this regard, presence may act as both means and end. In Santiago, spatial presence takes on a meaning and a form different from those in Palestine. As I have argued, Club Palestino represents in part an attempt at securing a continued presence of the Palestinian on Chilean soil. Protests and demonstrations in public space, however, make for another kind of presence altogether.

Keeping Palestine Alive

On one of the quieter afternoons during the Chilean winter of 2014, just a few days before the big march down La Alameda, Fernando talked to me once more about his commitment to Palestine and to a particular form of Palestinian resistance that he perceived himself and his peers to be practicing in Santiago. Evident in his take on this issue was the significance he afforded to a *continuing* Palestinian presence. As he explained, "We can keep our culture alive and Palestine alive in our society. The most important thing is to defend Palestine, from wherever." Ultimately, as Fernando put it, "the important thing is that we keep resisting. We have to have a tolerance for frustration. It's super frustrating. [But] we need to be the voice that Palestine doesn't have." Fernando's considerations on resistance not only point to the centrality of presence but highlight the work that goes into maintaining that presence, stubbornly keeping "Palestine alive" all the while constantly negotiating unwelcome presences and irritating reminders of other struggles. Supporting Palestine is still about making noise and calling attention to struggle and everyday life and resistance in the old land, but it is just as much about never letting that noise die down.[12]

That the temporal aspects of the ongoing Israeli encroachment upon Palestine should be central to Palestinian political engagement in diaspora is perhaps unsurprising. As Peteet (2008, 15) succinctly puts it, "Time, like space, has been critical to colonial rule in Palestine." At the same time, the still open-ended history of colonization brings a certain urgency to the matter of holding on to the past. Writing the history of the now became part of Palestinian practices of memory especially after the Second Intifada and draws continued purpose from the fact that the settler colonial project in Palestine is yet unfinished (Jayyusi 2007). Rather than repeated narratives of the past, then, narratives tied to the memory of the now have become central to the Palestinian struggle and reflect the sort of moving memory that I have dealt with here, a kind of memory that travels outward from Palestine and is kept in motion in places like Santiago.

These moving memories rely in part on social media for the circulation and reiteration of narratives and images of events very recently passed; they rely just as much on what, to a great extent, spurs on this sort of social media activity, namely repeated commemorative practices and the constant echoing of shared narratives. Together, ceremonial commemorations such as those that take place around the annual Nakba week and mnemonic connections forged via social media interplay with regularly repeated narratives of struggle and resistance to make for a dynamic mnemonic field that transcends physical location. As part of an effort to narrate and disseminate the Palestinian history of the now, the internet, and particularly social media, have undoubtedly come to play an important role, not least in Santiago (see Hanafi 2005; Hiller and Franz 2004). As I have aimed to show here, the onset of public demonstrations in July 2014 added an important layer to this effort among Palestinian Chileans engaging in *la causa*. At the same time, these demonstrations remained positioned within a context where belonging to a Palestinian establishment by and large meant being involved in efforts to construct boundaries that might ward off the uncomfortable aspects of past and present that dwelled in their immediate surroundings.

The marches for Gaza that took place in mid-2014 along various routes in Santiago served to disrupt the usual rhythm of the city and made established places into something else, twisting their meaning as people, their protest paraphernalia, and their noise moved through them. With the spectacularity, and with the visibility gained in bringing politics to the streets, these protests carried an intriguing potential as they took advantage of the public spaces available to them and used them to challenge the "normative world" (Cresswell 1996, 9; see Tawil-Souri 2012). These events were also inevitably tied to more overarching tendencies of despondency and a changing political imagination in the Chilean context.[13] When it comes to the cases of popular protest scrutinized in this chapter, Doreen Massey's (1995, 191) words ring true as she writes that "what has come together, in this place, now, is a conjunction of many histories and many spaces." At the same time, the presentness that these protests conjured up hinged to a great extent on the various absences that informed these very events (see Bille, Hastrup, and Sørensen 2010). During the pro-Palestine protests in which I took part, several absences were at play, not least the absences of establishment politics and the attempts to make absent the troublesome stuff of domestic politics altogether. These absences were tangible at the marches for Gaza, despite the fact that these attempts to make absent ultimately failed; the presence of both various groups of protesters and of past protest, as these demonstrations relied on modes of contention employed by others many times before, was unavoidable. Another absence, however, was perhaps even more instructive, namely that of what Palestinian Chilean marchers would refer to as *Palestina libre*: a free Palestine. This absence may be past or future, if not both, but it is without a doubt present. Palestinian memory politics in this context is largely aimed toward a future in which Palestine is returned to Palestinians. At the same time, it is always directed backward to a history of bereavement and thus an absence that reaches out from the depths of the past and into the present.

In this case, presence is not only about invoking the past in the now, but also about creating a space for presence in the future. By making noise and creating visibility for Palestine and the Palestinian cause in Santiago—thus creating openings in the mnemonic landscape of the city—Palestinian Chileans and sympathizers of *la causa* came together in pointing to a Palestinian reality free from violence and oppression (see also Springer 2014). They did so precisely by making use of the spaces and means available to them, drawing both on a repertoire of protest within public space and taking to the realm of social media, all the while negotiating shifting mnemonic boundaries. "How we imagine ourselves in the present is intimately linked to how we remember and represent ourselves in the past," write Owen J. Dwyer and Derek H. Alderman (2008, 172). Even further, how we imagine the future is intimately linked to how we understand and narrate both past and present, and vice versa. With the public protests against Operation Protective Edge, pasts and presents were brought together in interesting ways, connecting the Palestinian and the Chilean as the cleavages between them were challenged and their reminders kept on the move.

BORDERING AND UNBORDERING REMEMBRANCE

Remembering is one of the core modes of human engagement with the world. Through memory we perceive present realities and are equipped to imagine a variety of vivid futures. We sense through memory, and we make sense through memory. As a social phenomenon, memory aids us in collectively conceptualizing past, present, and future and allows us to envision the connections and fault lines that characterize our relations with one another. Memory is also work; by actively invoking certain memories and making present what is otherwise absent, we bring forth particular realities. In that regard, memory not only hinges on human labor but also works affectively to stir something in people and, in extension, works to affect the world. This is the crux of memory's political potential. It is also what I have tried to elucidate in this book. In exploring the politics of remembrance, I have argued that, as both a felt and practiced phenomenon, memory moves within, across, and beyond tangible and intangible borders that are inherently unstable and constantly shifting.

While insistently relating to what is absent, remembrance is simultaneously a deeply localized phenomenon; memories always appear to us under distinct circumstances in the here and now. At the same time, memory is not easily confined to any one location. It travels, it transgresses—it moves. This movement, in turn, revolves around affective engagements. In order to stay in motion as a living, breathing part of life, memory relies on its ability to move people by tapping into their sensory and emotional worlds.

Relatedly, remembrance seems to never quite escape recurring attempts at bordering and unbordering. Memory as an act of making present also, perhaps inevitably, involves the opposite: making absent, or reinforcing existing absences and bolstering the often invisible boundaries that persist, albeit tenuously, within geographies of memory. When people invoke certain absences, they often tend to actively keep others at bay. They tell certain stories rather than others. They shape their sensory worlds—through food, music, and more—to facilitate certain imaginaries over others. They build walls to separate bundles of memories and find themselves irritated when these walls are exposed as porous and largely unable to contain and confine. In parallel, others look to stories beyond their own and seek to dismantle walls of both the material and immaterial kind. The boundaries that are constructed and that, conversely, crack and crumble with these efforts speak directly to the movement of memory, though in no straightforward terms. Seeking to demarcate the territory of particular mnemonic worlds is in a sense also seeking to hold memory still and in place. To omit and occlude other memories is to render them unmoving. Yet it is rarely as simple as that in lived life. If memories rely on movement to stay alive and present, and people on both sides of any mnemonic border continuously move and are moved by memory, then stillness becomes an impossibility.

The tensions that come to the fore when people negotiate remembrance on the spectrum between stagnation and vibrancy, immobility and movement, confinement and free flow, are at the core of the problematics I have explored in this book. With the preceding forays into moving memory, I have aimed to shed light onto political imaginaries that intersect with geographical imaginaries, both of which are tightly connected to remembrance. In dealing with simultaneous attempts at coming to terms with the past and imagining alternative futures, the chapters of this book have each in their way tried to grapple with the interplay between efforts to move on from past trauma and remain open to futures imagined around the foundation of that very past. Here, the tensions surrounding these efforts are intensified by a context where colonialism and postcoloniality cohabit. In Palestine, settler colonialism is both an Israeli state-sanctioned political project and a felt reality on the ground. In Chile, the state of postcolonialism is near inseparable from the state of postdictatorship in its current-day expressions, the remnants of these two systems of governance having become enmeshed over time.

By approaching remembrance as a political force in the contemporary world through a diasporic lens, I have sought to explore a web of entanglements across and beyond spatiotemporal borders. From this position, a number of ambiguities become evident. Indeed, the case of those who work to remember Palestine in postdictatorship Chile highlights a set of paradoxes that is both analytically productive and politically significant. The first of these paradoxes is that, to the people whose narratives are at the core of this book, Palestine and the Palestinian cause are remembered and held present with more fervor and more consistency over time than any political reality pertaining to the Chilean context. At the same time, the stark political divisions that broadly characterize Chilean society are unmistakably reflected within and beyond the Palestinian establishment in Santiago. Another paradox follows from that, namely that the common cause that brings together Palestinian Chileans cannot and does not belong exclusively to a left-wing politics, as might otherwise be expected. Rather, this cause brings together, on the one hand, Palestinian Chileans of *la izquierda*, who see clear overlaps between oppressive measures used against Palestinians and ongoing state violence in Chile, and, on the other hand, the conservatives of *la derecha* whose concern with social justice and wider decolonial struggles is limited, to say the least. Following this, people associated with what I have called the Palestinian establishment in Santiago find themselves having to navigate a treacherous field of tension between a Chilean political landscape that is heavily charged as well as marked by conspicuous divisions and a Palestinian reality that may be playing out far from home but whose presence is nonetheless imposing and plays a weighty role in everyday life.

The dynamics of presence and absence inform various aspects of what has been discussed here and have thus come to form a steady undercurrent throughout the book. For Palestinians, a decades-long lack of recognition—along with what is often referred to as a threat of negation—has inevitably led to a heightened awareness of the importance of holding on to both a physical and a symbolic presence. Indeed, among people of Palestinian descent in Santiago, remembrance most often centers on the idea of "keeping Palestine alive" and present. In that sense, the commitment to diasporic remembrance has, at least to an extent, come to entail a paradoxical refusal to see the many ways in which past and present realities of the here and the elsewhere overlap.

In maintaining places dedicated to remembering Palestine, and in moving reminders through the city as was the case during the protests of July and August 2014, Palestinian memory not only travels between Palestine and Chile; it is also consistently kept in motion by those who, moved by it, have committed themselves to continuously activate and make noise about it. This commitment is palpable at commemorative events such as the ones marking the Nakba that I described in chapter 2, but also plays out spatially within what I have called the mnemonic landscape of the city.

In this landscape, tensions run high. Remembrance is largely ordered into more or less distinct bundles of memories that, in turn, have bearing on social and political life in the city and beyond. The continuation of systems upholding stark inequality as part of the legacy of dictatorship makes it difficult to ever entirely leave the past of authoritarian rule behind. Meanwhile, this is precisely what some people, not least within the Palestinian establishment, try to do. This state of things has of course not come out of nowhere. Following the onset of Palestinian immigration to Chile well over a century ago, a significant portion of the descendants of these first migrants have continuously worked to ensure a Palestinian presence along the streets of Santiago as well as within society at large. This presence naturally bears the imprint of those who have shaped it over time; it is a presence marked by both relative privilege and experiences of discrimination, poverty, and hardship in the early decades of settlement as well as, more recently, the ascent up the socioeconomic ladder by a significant number of Palestinian Chilean families. Additionally, despite few Palestinian immigrants and their descendants having lived through the Nakba of 1948, this unfinished catastrophe has had enormous bearing on the formation of a Palestinian—rather than Arab—diasporic community in the Chilean context. This combination of factors seems to have resulted in the making of what Laila called "their own bubble"—a distinctly Palestinian sphere pivoting around the Federación Palestina de Chile and Club Palestino, perhaps the most well-guarded place of Palestinian memory in Santiago.

In including diasporic remembrance in an exploration of Santiago's landscape of memory, we are faced with simultaneous but sometimes perhaps mutually exclusive attempts at coming to terms with multiple pasts while imagining alternative futures on the foundation of those very pasts. Within the city of Santiago itself, Palestine is represented—made present—within various places. Whereas Patronato represents early Palestinianness in Chile—poverty and hardship, but also entrepreneurship and hard work—Club Palestino represents a Palestinian success story of moving up and gaining wealth, not least in terms of land. When protesters marched down La Alameda to call for an end to the violence in Gaza in mid-2014, they too brought a Palestinian presence to the heart of the city, even if only in passing. All these places have in one way or another served to secure and maintain—for shorter or longer periods of time—a Palestinian presence in the Chilean capital. At the same time, they are solidly grounded within a landscape formed by layers of contentious pasts.

Unevenly developed as it is, Santiago is at once a palimpsest, written over with remnants and reminders of different times, and a contested space where traces of past conflict are intermittently sought to be erased or accentuated. This has only become all the clearer in the wake of the 2019 Chilean popular uprising—*el estallido social*—during which the streets and plazas of the city were once more used to display people's dissatisfaction with the lingering status quo, bringing to light the continued significance of past politics to everyday life in the present. While certain memories have materialized in the form of monuments, memorials, and other sites of memory scattered across the city, their presence in the landscape is precarious and subject to investment. At the same time, although many of these reminders call attention to the state violence carried out during dictatorship, the northeastern parts of the city—home to Club Palestino and a large part of the Palestinian establishment—bear few material traces of this sort of remembrance.

Within these surroundings, retreating to diasporic memory and building distinctly Palestinian places serve to complicate an already rough and bumpy mnemonic landscape. By building walls—of both the brick-and-mortar and symbolic kinds—and trying to abandon memories of a disturbing Chilean past for the sake of highlighting a Palestinian past at once distant, recent, and unfinished, the largely conservative forces within the Palestinian establishment in Santiago do not in fact break with the order of this landscape, but rather reinforce its existing unevenness by simply adding further bundles of memories to its already complex makeup.

The boundaries I have traced along the preceding pages are both real and imagined, material and immaterial, sometimes part of the physical landscape and sometimes simply present as lines cutting through sociopolitical worlds. No matter how they present themselves, however, these boundaries tend to be porous and malleable. Despite efforts to avoid mnemonic amalgamation, unwelcome reminders of other unfinished pasts often rear their heads, causing irritation among those who would prefer to stay unbothered and unaffected. Among others, Tarek expressed this irritation clearly, not least by describing how he felt unmoved by struggles and political causes beyond the Palestinian. At the same time, irritation is just as much an emotional response as the kind that spurs people into action. Absences can thus be both agitating in their refusal to stay absent and troublesome in what they bring with them, making them doubly uneasy.

The demonstrations that were organized and carried out during Operation Protective Edge made this particularly clear as they called attention to the Palestinian struggle within a distinct Chilean context. The marches for Gaza were solidly located in this context not only because they took place within the physical space of that context, but because they linked the Palestinian cause with wider political tendencies—not least disillusionment with government politics—and a history of popular protest. At least since Allende's rise to power, Chilean politics have developed along a sharply drawn divide between opposing visions for the future. When his socialist ideals violently collided with the staunch neoliberalism that came to be implemented by Pinochet and his junta, it set the tone for decades to come. In today's Chile, politics are still very much marked by the ruptures created by opposing understandings of the past and disparate imaginings of the future. The contentiousness of the past has perhaps rendered unavoidable a certain culture of oblivion, but at the same time, the past currently informs a wide range of protests and other forms of dissent. Growing pressure on the political establishment by way of popular mobilizations will most likely continue to alter the direction of Chilean politics into the near future in a way that could eventually mean a radical shift of course.

At the protest marches described in chapter 5 in particular, there was no escaping efforts at solidarity put forth by those who came along to show support for Gaza as non-Palestinian people and organizations, with political parties and football fans joining the ranks of the Palestinian Chilean institutions and groups represented. In a sense, the marches and manifestations for Gaza compressed past and future into the present by drawing on both Palestinian and Chilean histories while opening up for a particular future collectively envisioned. Yet while both memory projects look to the future, they most often seem to run parallel to each other without intersecting, at least on the surface. However, as became particularly obvious during this period, the very relationship between memories that are kept present, in motion, and those excluded and obscured is unnerving in that the potential for boundary-challenging spillover is always present.

These events likewise foregrounded how remembering can entail engagement with mnemonic registers that are rooted elsewhere and thus do not spring from either lived memory or postmemory. The memories that travel from Palestine to the Chilean capital are manifold, diverse, and pertain to a past both far gone and recently lived; at the same time, they revolve around familiar motifs: struggle, resistance, and belonging to the land. Those who have been able to travel to Palestine themselves, like Fernando, bring home their own memories in the wake of witnessing the occupation and its effects on Palestinian everyday life, and the few Palestinian Chileans who migrated themselves, of course, bring their own lived experiences with them. Most people, however, rely on mediated and repeatedly narrated accounts to form memories of Palestine. These memories are formed through collective commemorative practices and via the more informal sharing of stories between family members, friends, and peers. Importantly, however, social media have come to play an enormously significant role in the immediate transferral, translation, and transfiguration of memories that move from one place to another and undergo subtle changes as they are taken in within varying contexts—transcending any fixed meaning. The underlying principle remains whether we look at images shared online or narratives repeated at annual ceremonies to commemorate events that happened elsewhere, long ago: memories do not tend to stay in place.

The paradoxes described above and the ways in which they are managed as part of everyday life tell us something about the complex sociopolitical workings of remembrance in the contemporary world, not least in settings marked by past or present settler colonial projects. The early decades of the twenty-first century have marked a gradual shift in how we acknowledge, activate, and archive the past. Now more than ever before, memory is a trans-spatial phenomenon. Exploring the fault lines between particular bundles of memories holds significant lessons on the ongoing bordering and unbordering of the world, as does identifying the breaches in these bundles through which connections are made. These lessons I have only just begun to grasp with this work, and many questions remain unanswered.

As a theoretical intervention, the idea that memory moves within and between people, times, and spaces urges us to take note of how the past is sought to be confined and released, held in place or let go to travel where it may. It also reminds us of the affective qualities of memory and how important they are in relation to politics of remembrance. For many of the people I worked with in Santiago, remembering matters because they *feel* that it matters. The emotional, sometimes visceral, responses they experience in relation to past and present Palestinian realities move them into action and remind them that memory—in the basic sense of *keeping present*—holds political potential. In turn, these responses are wrapped up in ambiguous and shifting perceptions of proximity and distance; what might otherwise appear to be close at hand can seem distant, even absent, while faraway worlds are invited into the here and now. Finally, and perhaps most importantly, tending to how memory moves alerts us to the porosity of the borders constructed around remembrance and the futility of attempts to keep it from seeping through the cracks of whatever material or immaterial constructions are built to protect it.

Notes

INTRODUCTION

1. All names have been changed for the sake of anonymity, apart from the names of people who appear in this book in their capacity as professionals or public figures.

2. The characteristic Palestinian scarf in black and white, made especially popular by Yassir Arafat as his trademark and still seen as one of the strongest symbols of Palestinian resistance.

3. See, e.g., Chomsky (2014).

4. Studies of Palestinian diasporicity and Palestinian life in exile are nonetheless manifold and have informed many of the considerations put forth here. Most of these studies deal with the realities of life in exile for Palestinian refugees and focus especially on refugee camp dwellers in Arab countries, particularly Lebanon (e.g., Allan 2005, 2013; Peteet 2005; Sayigh [1979] 2007, 2013; Schiocchet 2013). A number of scholars have sought to expand research on Palestinian diasporicity to include a wider variety of contexts, from Europe and Australia to the Americas (e.g., Abdulhadi 2004; Gren 2015; Hammer 2005; Kublitz 2011; Mason 2007; Mavroudi 2008; Schulz 2003). At the same time, the traditional approach to diaspora as first and foremost a social formation has been widely critiqued for reasons that do not require repetition here (see, e.g., Anthias 1998; Brubaker 2005; Sökefeld 2006; Soysal 2000).

5. Officially Avenida Libertador General Bernardo O'Higgins.

6. I have dealt with the complex heritage of Patronato in more detail elsewhere (Schwabe 2021).

7. Although it is beyond the scope of this book, I have discussed the political implications of this institution elsewhere (see Schwabe 2018b).

8. According to several people I talked to, it was not uncommon for Orthodox Palestinians to convert to Catholicism, but a large number stuck to their denomination and were eventually able to practice their faith in Santiago at two Orthodox churches with a strong Palestinian profile: the Catedral Ortodoxa San Jorge in Patronato and the Iglesia Ortodoxa de la Santísima Virgen María, located in the district of Providencia.

9. Even as far north as the United States, immigrants from the Ottoman Empire were simply called "Turks" (Shohat and Alsultany 2013, 8; see also Rebolledo Hernández 1994).

10. The complete guide is available online at http://www.memoriachilena.cl/602/w3-article-9760.html.

11. Other texts that deal with Chile's Palestinians include Juan Antonio Pacheco's (2006) article on the Arab press, Heba El-Attar's (2011) comparative analysis of the Palestinian and Jewish press, and Jeffrey Lesser and Raanan Rein's (2011) introduction to the special issue of the *Journal of Latin American and Caribbean Ethnic Studies* in which El-Attar's article is featured. Some earlier studies focus on the "political emergence" of Arab Chileans (Bray 1962) or deal with the wider issue of Arab immigration to and settlement in South and Central America (e.g., Abugattas 1982; Klich and Lesser 1998).

12. Meanwhile, the contentious nature of memory itself is dealt with in various ways within scholarship on the region (see, e.g., Bilbija and Payne 2011; Conte 2015; Lazzara and Unruh 2009; Saona 2014).

13. Using the 2019 Chilean uprising as an entry point for reflecting on the past, Romina A. Green Rioja describes her grandmother's memories of the coup of 1973 and the time that followed—her sadness at witnessing the presidential palace attacked and her fear when the military raided the family home—and aptly writes, "Those memories are so vivid that I sometimes believe them to be my own" (2021, 5; see also Gómez-Barris 2010; Hite 2012).

14. See also Crownshaw, Kilby, and Rowland (2010) for various considerations on the future of memory.

15. To a great extent I follow Edward S. Casey's (1997, xiii) lead, as he insists that *place* contains elements of "identity, character, nuance, history" (see also Adams, Hoelscher, and Till 2001; Cresswell 1996; Low 2009). Following from that, I take *space* to first and foremost designate the realm within which places come to be, although this realm is much more than a mere container, more than something juxtaposed as meaningless against the meaningfulness of place (Massey 2005, 6; see also Malpas [1999] 2004; Thomas 1993).

16. Outside of the capital city, other such places have undergone similar transitions; in 2016, the highly controversial former torture and detention center known as Colonia Dignidad, located a few hours south of Santiago, was adopted as a national monument (*monumento nacional*) following years of advocacy by victims' relatives (Consejo de Monumentos Nacionales de Chile 2016; see also Falconer 2008).

17. See Andermann (2015), C. Collins (2011), Hite (2012), Klep (2012), and Till (2003) for further perspectives on memorials and the politics of "places of memory" in Santiago and beyond.

1. TOGETHER APART

1. Chile consolidated Free Trade Agreements with the European Union, the European Free Trade Association, and South Korea in 2003, and with China and Japan in 2006 and 2007 respectively (Alexander 2009, 15–16).

2. According to Patricia Arancibia Clavel, Roberto Arancibia Clavel, and Isabel Jara Hinojosa (2010, 55), however, almost all the immigrants who came to Chile from Ottoman-ruled Palestine did so by crossing the Andes from Mendoza on the Argentinian border. The mountains were commonly traversed by mule up until the cross-Andean railway was inaugurated in 1910. This version resonates with both other written sources (e.g., Agar and Saffie 2005) and some family accounts as they were presented to me.

3. September 18, often referred to simply as the *dieciocho*, has been the national Chilean holiday ever since the year 1811 when, on that date, the first independent assembly gathered in Santiago, professing "cautious autonomism" from the Spanish crown (Stern 2010, 33; Collier and Sater 2004, 33).

4. Indeed, as Kårtveit (2014, 198) points out, even in Bethlehem there is a prevalent notion that emigrants from the area "have been smart, industrious and very successful in their endeavors, wherever they have settled."

5. See once more, e.g., Arancibia Clavel, Arancibia Clavel, and Jara Hinojosa (2010); Baeza (2014a). According to Manzar Foroohar (2011, 10), Palestinians came to fill a void in the economy of the Americas. As he writes, "Iberian colonialism had brought to the New World a socioeconomic system based on large landownership and a landed aristocracy, and the upper class had a deep disdain for commercial and banking activities." With that, Faroohar (2011, 10) argues, the Palestinians who came to Latin America were needed to respond to the growing demands of a quickly developing market economy, which could not go without merchants and industrialists. However, as Palestinians came to assume the positions no one else seemed to want, they exposed themselves to the disdain of those who remained stuck to the old ways and considered the commercial arena less than respectable

(see Rebolledo Hernández 1994). Along the way, as Palestinian businesses flourished and their owners gained wealth, these immigrant traders and entrepreneurs faced intensified discrimination throughout Latin America, as they came to pose a direct threat to the economic status of the old elite (Faroohar 2011; Baeza 2014a). Thus, much of early Palestinian life in Chile and beyond was marked by an awkward "tension between economic desirability and social undesirability" (Klich and Lesser 1996, 8). A similar understanding to a great extent characterized common accounts of Palestinian immigration to Chile and Latin America during my time in Santiago.

6. According to Baeza (2014a), with reference to the registers of Chile's Syrian-Palestinian Commercial Association, exactly 147 plants were established with "Arab funds" within a five-year period in the mid-1930s.

7. In a fascinating book, Peter Winn (1986) follows the workers at the Yarur cotton mill, founded by Bethlehem-born Juan Yarur Lolas, along "Chile's road to socialism" (see also Baeza 2014a).

8. The Second Palestinian Intifada (or uprising)—also known as the Al-Aqsa Intifada—took place between 2000 and 2005 (see Baroud 2006; Norman 2010).

9. See http://www.federacionpalestina.cl/.

10. See, e.g., Rigby (2015, 17–23).

11. While the General Union of Palestinian Students has, from the outset, been a transnational endeavor, the Chilean UGEP did not engage actively with other chapters of the organization. In the words of Fernando, a member of the UGEP leadership, "the General Union of Palestinian Students is all over the world, but first [before engaging with them], we need to work more in Chile, to create ties with people in the regions [outside of Santiago] more so than in other countries."

12. At the same time, as several UGEP members were quick to point out, their organization is first and foremost, as the name implies, a union of *Palestinian* students and should not necessarily expand beyond that.

13. It is, however, my impression that UGEP has increasingly been forging ties to external actors since my time in Santiago; for instance, the leaders of the organization expressed their solidarity with protesters during 2019's mass protests that became known as *el estallido social*—the social explosion—in Chile, and have likewise been voicing solidarity with feminist and indigenous movements via their social media, although not without some backlash.

14. See www.colegioarabe.cl.

15. One of the school's older students estimated that around three quarters of the student body is Palestinian Chilean, but I have not been able to find any statistical evidence to back up this claim.

16. *Cuica* is a common Chilean slang expression (or "*chilenismo*") denoting a person from the upper class, a snob, or someone who is stuck-up.

17. Las Condes is itself located in the very northeast of Santiago, at the foot of the Andes mountains, and is, in its furthest corners, thus far removed from the city's other, poorer, areas.

18. See Foroohar (2011) and Baeza (2014a).

19. The First Intifada was a popular Palestinian uprising that began in late 1987 and has been called "one of the most grassroots-based mobilizations in the Middle East in the past century" (Bayat 2013, 6; see also Rigby 2015). Interestingly, both the First and Second Intifada had tangible effects in Chile, where the uprisings spurred on wide mobilization, especially among young Palestinian Chileans—the first coinciding with the establishment of UGEP in the 1980s and the second with the revival of UGEP in the early 2000s.

20. Although not as impressive in numbers as their Palestinian Chilean counterparts, Jewish Chileans are a prominent part of Chile's demographic makeup and are to a great

extent as committed to the Israeli cause as many Palestinian Chileans are to the Palestinian (see Guiskin 2013; El-Attar 2011). Apart from debates and sometimes head-on confrontations in the media, the Palestinian Chilean and Jewish establishments have very few formal ties or common platforms. Between 2006 and 2008, however, an attempt at informal conversation between so-called Arab and Jewish youth in Santiago was made. Spearheaded by two professors—a descendant of Syrian immigrants and a son of Jewish immigrants from Europe—the project brought together a group of young people to engage in "intercultural dialogue" (see Agar Corbinos and Magendzo Kolstrein 2009). Although described to me by several people who partook in the project as a good experience, it had not had a very lasting effect. By the time of my fieldwork, another initiative to encourage sustained dialogue between people of Palestinian and Jewish descent had been kicked off in Santiago, and a small group of about half a dozen people—calling themselves Consenso Chileno por la Paz Palestino-Israelí (Chilean Consensus for Palestinian-Israeli Peace) were still meeting regularly when I left in August 2014, albeit with very little involvement from or attention paid by the Palestinian establishment. More than animosity, this tendency was wrapped up in staunch rejection of efforts to "normalize" Israeli-Palestinian relations. This antinormalization stance was common and reflected overarching Palestinian efforts to continuously call attention to the harsh reality of occupation and oppression, a reality not easily improved by friendly dialogue. Indeed, dialogue within this perspective was and continues to be seen as potentially veiling of the violence endured by Palestinians on a daily basis (see Darweish and Rigby 2015, 112; Stein and Swedenburg 2005, 14). Before any real dialogue could be established, claimed one of the people I spoke to about it, "we need the Jewish community [in Chile] to say that they don't support Israel. We need them to say 'enough, but seriously, enough' [*basta, pero basta en serio*]."

21. During a later conversation, Andrea echoed Ana's viewpoints: "Obviously the Palestinian cause can't be a right-wing cause! The right wing protects people's pockets, but Palestinian politics is not right-wing politics. It's one big contradiction."

22. Although efforts at solidarity work between Palestinian associations and, e.g., Mapuche organizations in Chile were often put to a halt early on during this time, international solidarity and transnational political engagement remain a big part of the Palestinian struggle—though one it will not be possible to delve into here. One of the most talked about cases of transnational and trans-movement solidarity in recent years has been Black-Palestinian solidarity, especially in the wake of the US Black Lives Matter movement and 2014's Operation Protective Edge in Gaza (see, e.g., blackforpalestine.com, as well as Erekat and Hill 2019; Feldman 2015; Lubin 2014 for context). See also Abdulhadi (2004) on pro-Palestine activism outside Palestine.

23. It is worth noting that Laila's take on Allende's politics as discriminatory stood out and was not shared by others I discussed the issue with.

2. STAGING THE PAST

1. The *dabke* is an Arab folk dance that has come to take on a particular meaning among Palestinian Chileans and that is often invoked as a symbol of Palestinian resistance (see Kaschl 2003). As a mode of commemoration, the *dabke* shares similarities with the Chilean *cueca*, a traditional dance that is not only an important part of the annual *fiestas patrias* but has also been employed in commemorative performances, perhaps most notably in the form of the *cueca sola*, whereby women dance alone and thus point to the absence of their dance partners, most often victims of dictatorship (see Green Rioja 2021).

2. The speech was given in Spanish and is reproduced here in my translated version.

3. The full tweet reads as follows: "Yo soy esa cara de nana, esa cara parecida a la tuya, pequeña y pelo negro, yo soy esa cara con rasgos que parece incomodar tu clase desclasada" (@anatijoux, March 31, 2014).

4. See MacWilliam (2014) on the tension between support for Palestine and indigenous rights in Chile.

5. The direct influence of the US government on these developments has been treated in depth by many (e.g., Gómez-Barris 2009, 2010; Harmer 2013; Kaplan 2004; Paley 2001) but is not of crucial importance in the context of this book. However, it is worth noting that the political developments in Chile from the late 1960s onward did not stand alone but were rather part of much more wide-reaching developments.

6. According to Steve Stern (2010, 36), "well-informed estimates range from 200,000 to 400,000" Chileans who went into exile, mainly for political, but some also for economic reasons; according to Teresa Meade (2001, 138n7), however, UN estimates claim that around a million Chileans left the country from 1973 until the mid-1980s.

7. Although it remains unknown how many of these centers existed throughout Chile, as many as eighty-seven centers are believed to have been located in Santiago alone (Meade 2001, 127).

8. See Gómez-Barris (2009), Meade (2001), Stern (2010), and Taylor (2011) for more in-depth discussions of some of these sites.

9. As Carlos Huneeus (2007, 272) has pointed out, however, the results garnered by the Chicago Boys were "uneven: neoliberal policies led Chile into its worst recession of the century" in the early 1980s.

10. Officially Pontificia Universidad Católica de Chile.

11. As Julia Paley (2001, 7) writes, the military coup "introduced one of the most comprehensive free market restructurings ever attempted worldwide." This restructuring of the Chilean economy into one based on consumption and the free market has had massive consequences across the board. First and foremost, it has resulted in an intense and fast-paced escalation of economic inequality, an escalation with consequences not only to economic fault lines in current-day Chile (see Han 2012).

12. See also Frazier (2007, 81) on countermemory in Chile.

13. The other two were held at the University of Chile and at Club Palestino respectively.

14. See Massad (2015).

3. UNEASY ABSENCES

1. Indeed, the same could be said for Palestinian Chileans specifically; both Andrea and others had made a habit of joining the big Friday protests at the informally renamed Plaza de la Dignidad—formerly Plaza Italia—by the time I last visited the city in early 2020.

2. In a 2016 article in *La Tercera* it was reported that more than twelve thousand people gave up their membership of a political party in Chile during the course of one year from December 2014 to December 2015 (Álvarez and Carrasco 2016).

3. Rather than a democracy per se, Paley points out, what Chile is left with after democracy has popularly been referred to as "*democracia ristringida* (restricted democracy), *democracia copular* (elite democracy), *democracia lite* (low-fat democracy), and *democracia entre comillas* (democracy in quotation marks)" (2001, 3; italics in the original).

4. Despite the violence of the dictatorship era, Pinochet enjoyed remarkable support during his time as head of state, and even to this day many remember his rule as essentially good for the people and the nation. According to Stern (2010, 90), a 1993 survey showed that, within what he classifies as the Chilean upper-class segment, just over 53 percent agreed with the statement that "on 11 September 73 Chile was liberated from Marxism." Interestingly, the rhetoric of salvation at the brink of disaster is, according to Loveman and Lira (2007, 46), one that has been employed by "all contenders for control" in the Chilean context over the course of centuries.

5. Meanwhile, most efforts at reckoning with Pinochet and his allies took place outside the courtroom and focused on a "soft" approach to dealing with the past, namely through testimony, not least within the domain of truth and reconciliation commissions (see Stern 2010; Klep 2012).

6. At the time of Pinochet's 1998 retirement as army commander and repositioning as lifetime senator, criminal complaints began being made against him, piling up in the following months until reaching 158 cases by the time his immunity was stripped by the Chilean supreme court in 2000 (Stern 2010, 248–49). The formal opening of the International Criminal Court (ICC) in 2002 marked the early twenty-first century as a time that would be centered on justice and coming to terms with past atrocities on a global scale. In 1998, Chile had been one among the states that signed the Rome treaty, offering official support for the establishment of the ICC (see Stern 2010, 165, 221). More than a decade later, Palestine was to join the ICC in early 2015 (see, e.g., Hadid and Simons 2015). Although Pinochet himself narrowly escaped prosecution for reasons of deteriorating health, other high-ranking officers were condemned following a range of court cases.

7. See Schwabe (2018a) for further discussion of this.

4. WHERE MEMORY MOVES

1. Fernando was not the only person I talked with about traveling to Palestine, and many expressed having experienced something similar. Without exception, those who had not been to Palestine expressed a strong desire to someday be able to travel there. Most of these people, both young and old, had simply not had the financial means to travel and were often people who had not gone to Colegio Árabe and did not have very strong ties to Club Palestino or other Palestinian Chilean institutions. Among those who had made the trip, however, some had been turned away at the Israeli border and were forced to travel back to Chile directly. Indeed, several stories of denied entry were well known and circulated within Palestinian Chilean circles. First and foremost, these stories were brought up to underline the harsh reality of occupation as felt even for Chilean citizens of Palestinian descent and, often in these cases, Palestinian-sounding names.

2. Operación Retorno (Operation Return) is an annual trip organized by the Federación Palestina de Chile and aimed at Palestinian Chileans who want to (re)visit the land of their ancestors. The trip is not funded by the Federation, however, and those without the means to travel are thus automatically excluded.

3. Importantly, in both cases, narratives and notions of the past continue their orientation beyond the earliest days of the Nakba. Although his paternal grandparents only came to Chile in the 1950s, Fernando's engagement with Palestine hinges on memories that go back to the time when the other side of his family and so many other Palestinians made their way to South America. Likewise, Sayigh highlights "the continuity between the struggle in Palestine before the Disaster, and the struggle outside it afterwards" ([1979] 2007, 4).

4. Nadia Abu El-Haj examines these "facts on the ground" from a different angle by scrutinizing the importance of archaeological endeavors for Israel's "colonial-national historical imagination" (2001, 2). Meanwhile, Nina Gren (2015, 237) has written on the importance of constructing Palestinian houses within this landscape and argued that creating Palestinian "facts on the ground"—or what might be called counter-facts that challenge Israeli-made changes to the landscape—has become a strategy of defiance, even for Sweden-based Palestinians who, despite not living in Palestine, make it a priority to build homes, in the literal as well as figurative sense, in the old land.

5. Importantly, for many Palestinians in Palestine, staying put is a consequence of imposed limitations on movement rather than a political choice (see Kelly 2009).

6. See also Schwabe (2017). Of course, not only Palestinian places but Palestinian bodies play a significant role in that regard. Although beyond the scope of this book, others have dealt with the contentious politics of the Palestinian body from different angles (e.g., Busse 2015; Butler 2015; Ryan 2016; Seikaly 2014).

7. See Pearlman (2011) as well as Stein and Swedenburg (2005) on the relationship between politics, nonviolence, and popular culture in Palestine.

8. Part of its infamy rests on the very size of the operation that took place there during dictatorship: around "5000 prisoners passed through Villa Grimaldi, and it is known that 240 of them were killed or disappeared" (Meade 2001, 125; see Gómez-Barris 2009, 38).

9. See Edensor (2008) and Trigg (2012) on similarly haunted places.

5. SEEING AND BELIEVING

1. And, although given much less attention for relative lack of intensity, the West Bank.

2. According to people I knew who had been around when the student movement started regaining traction in 2011, downtown Santiago "felt like a war zone" during protests, with police using both tear gas and water cannons almost indiscriminately as if, as one person put it to me, "it's just what they do." The response of the Chilean police, the so-called *carabineros*, is however beyond the scope of this text.

3. The Penguin Revolution (*Revolución pingüina*)—named as such with reference to the look of the protesters' school uniforms—took off in April 2006 and saw over a million students mobilized for equal access to free, quality education in the biggest uprising since the end of dictatorship (Chovanec and Benitez 2008).

4. Rather ironically, a young Palestinian Chilean woman told me that she had been told off by fellow protesters when she brought a Palestinian flag to a student protest. Thus, UGEP and the establishment as such do not seem to be alone in rejecting signifiers that might seem a distraction to the primary cause of any given demonstration.

5. This attack was widely reported on and condemned, rendering it perhaps the most controversial moment of the 2014 incursion. Later on, the Israeli military conducted an investigation into the incident and ultimately exonerated itself (see Beaumont 2015).

6. The dynamics of "cyberculture," "cyber colonialism," and "cyberactivism" in Palestine and beyond have been explored in more detail by others (e.g., Khalili 2005; Tawil-Souri and Aouragh 2014).

7. See also Van Dijck (2007) on memory and media.

8. As Jeffrey Hou points out, however, in a world of "hyper-security and surveillance, new forms of control in public space have curtailed freedom of movement and expression and greatly limited the activities and meanings of contemporary public space" (2010, 3).

9. Notably, Ilan Pappé (2006) has made the case for using the term "ethnic cleansing" to describe the same processes of displacement that are at stake in Hanafi's argument. For Hanafi, however, ethnic cleansing is only one aspect of an overarching process of spaciocide that also includes the "mass destruction of space" as well as a "a growing apartheid system" (2012, 191–192).

10. This invisibility is, perhaps paradoxically, tied to the rendering visible of Palestinian life through Israeli surveillance and control (Azoulay 2013; Khalili 2010; Selwyn 2001; Swedenburg 2003).

11. See Fabian ([1983] 2002, 29–30) on time and "political physics."

12. Closely tied to the promotion of the Palestinian cause is a counterpoint to such promotion, namely the boycott of any product or institution that might in some way help sustain the Israeli occupation of Palestine. During my time in Santiago, a small group of people had formed an unofficial coordination committee to oversee efforts at boycott

among Palestinian Chileans as well among the Chilean public more generally. This group considered themselves part of the transnational movement that has come to be known as BDS (Boycott, Divestment, and Sanctions) and mostly disseminated BDS news and updates via social media, seeking to promote practices of boycott (see Bröning 2011; Goldenberg 2015; Hallward 2013). The student organization FECH (Federación de Estudiantes de la Universidad de Chile) has likewise been behind similar initiatives to promote BDS from within the University of Chile (see *El Ciudadano* 2015).

13. General despondency aside, the Palestinian cause is not entirely absent within the political establishment in Chile. Several Palestinian Chileans hold seats in parliament and local councils—Daniel Jadue being but one example of a successful politician—and represent both right- and left-wing parties. Moreover, according to a 2014 article, the Chile-Palestine Inter-Parliamentary Group in the Chilean parliament included an impressive 46 out of a total of 120 members of the House of Deputies, making it "currently the largest of binational friendship groups" (Baeza 2014b). While the presence of Palestinian Chileans and the Palestinian cause within the Chilean legislature is a topic that deserves further scrutiny, it is not the focus of my research.

References

Abdulhadi, Rabab. 2004. "Activism and Exile: Palestinianness and the Politics of Solidarity." In *Local Actions: Cultural Activism, Power, and Public Life in America*, edited by Melissa Checker and Maggie Fishman, 231–53. New York: Columbia University Press.

Abu El-Haj, Nadia. 2001. *Facts on the Ground: Archaeological Practice and Territorial Self-Fashioning in Israeli Society*. Chicago: University of Chicago Press.

Abugattas, Juan. 1982. "The Perception of the Palestinian Question in Latin America." *Journal of Palestine Studies* 11 (3): 117–28.

Abu-Lughod, Lila. 2007. "Return to Half-Ruins: Memory, Postmemory, and Living History in Palestine." In *Nakba: Palestine, 1948, and the Claims of Memory*, edited by Ahmad H. Sa'di and Lila Abu-Lughod, 77–104. New York: Columbia University Press.

Abu-Lughod, Lila, and Ahmad H. Sa'di. 2007. "Introduction: The Claims of Memory." In *Nakba: Palestine, 1948, and the Claims of Memory*, edited by Ahmad H. Sa'di and Lila Abu-Lughod, 1–24. New York: Columbia University Press.

Adams, Paul C., Steven Hoelscher, and Karen E. Till. 2001. "Place in Context: Rethinking Humanist Geographies." In *Textures of Place: Exploring Humanist Geographies*, edited by Paul C. Adams, Steven Hoelscher, and Karen E. Till, xiii–xxxiii. Minneapolis: University of Minnesota Press.

Agar, Lorenzo, and Nicole Saffie. 2005. "Chilenos de origen árabe: La fuerza de las raíces." *Revista Miscelánea de Estudios Árabes y Hebraicos* 54:3–27.

Agar Corbinos, Lorenzo, and Abraham Magendzo Kolstrein, eds. 2009. *Diálogo intercultural: Comunidad Árabe y Judía en Chile*. Santiago: Ideas.

Aguilera, Carolina. 2015. "Memories and Silences of a Segregated City: Monuments and Political Violence in Santiago, Chile, 1970–1991." *Memory Studies* 8 (1): 102–14.

Ahmed, Sara. 1999. "Home and Away: Narratives of Migration and Estrangement." *International Journal of Cultural Studies* 2 (3): 329–47.

Alexander, William L. 2009. "Introduction: Enduring Contradictions of the Neoliberal State in Chile." In *Lost in the Long Transition: Struggles for Social Justice in Neoliberal Chile*, edited by William L. Alexander, 1–38. Lanham, MD: Lexington Books.

Allan, Diana. 2005. "Mythologising Al-Nakba: Narratives, Collective Identity and Cultural Practice among Palestinian Refugees in Lebanon." *Oral History* 33 (1): 47–56.

———. 2013. "Commemorative Economies and the Politics of Solidarity in Shatila Camp." *Humanity* 4 (1): 133–48.

Allen, Lori A. 2009. "Martyr Bodies in the Media: Human Rights, Aesthetics, and the Politics of Immediation in the Palestinian Intifada." *American Ethnologist* 36 (1): 161–80.

Álvarez, M. E., and F. Carrasco. 2016. "Todos los partidos políticos perdieron militantes en 2015." *La Tercera*, February 13. http://www.latercera.com/noticia/politica/2016/02/674–668212-9-militantes-en-fuga.shtml.

Álvarez, Paolo. 2011. "La Chimba del Valle del Mapocho: Historia de una alteridad en construcción (siglos XVI–XIX)." *Espacios* 1:19–42.

Andermann, Jens. 2015. "Placing Latin American Memory: Sites and the Politics of Mourning." *Memory Studies* 8 (1): 3–8.

Angell, Alan. 2007. *Democracy after Pinochet: Politics, Parties and Elections in Chile.* London: Institute for the Study of the Americas.

Anthias, Floya. 1998. "Evaluating 'Diaspora': Beyond Ethnicity?" *Sociology* 32 (3): 557–80.

Arancibia Clavel, Patricia, Roberto Arancibia Clavel, and Isabel Jara Hinojosa. 2010. *Tras la huella de los Árabes en Chile: Una historia de esfuerza e integración.* Santiago: Instituto Democracia y Mercado.

Arendt, Hannah. 1958. *The Human Condition.* Chicago: University of Chicago Press.

Assmann, Aleida. 2018. "One Land and Three Narratives: Palestinian Sites of Memory in Israel." *Memory Studies* 11 (3): 287–300.

Assmann, Aleida, and Linda Shortt, eds. 2012. *Memory and Political Change.* Basingstoke, UK: Palgrave Macmillan.

Augé, Marc. 2004. *Oblivion.* Translated by Marjolijn de Jager. Minneapolis: University of Minnesota Press.

Axel, Brian Keith. 2004. "The Context of Diaspora." *Cultural Anthropology* 19 (1): 26–60.

Azoulay, Ariella. 2013. "When a Demolished House Becomes a Public Square." In *Imperial Debris: On Ruins and Ruination*, edited by Ann Laura Stoler, 194–224. Durham, NC: Duke University Press.

Bachelard, Gaston. (1958) 2014. *The Poetics of Space.* Translated by Maria Jolas. New York: Penguin Books.

Baeza, Cecilia. 2005. "Les Palestiniens du Chili: De la conscience diasporique à la mobilisation transnationale." *Revue d'études palestiniennes* 95:51–87.

———. 2011. "Women in Arab-Palestinian Associations in Chile: Long Distance Nationalism and Gender Mixing." *Al-Raida* 133–34:18–32.

———. 2014a. "Palestinians in Latin America: Between Assimilation and Long-Distance Nationalism." *Journal of Palestine Studies* 43 (2): 59–72.

———. 2014b. "Solidaridad con Gaza." *Middle East Research and Information Project*, July 22. http://www.merip.org/solidaridad-con-gaza.

Bahloul, Joëlle. 1996. *The Architecture of Memory: A Jewish-Muslim Household in Colonial Algeria, 1937–1962.* Translated by Catherine du Peloux Ménagé. Cambridge: Cambridge University Press.

Bakhtin, Mikhail. 1981. *The Dialogic Imagination: Four Essays.* Edited by Michael Holquist, translated by Caryl Emerson and Michael Holquist. Austin: University of Texas Press.

Barder, Alexander D. 2013. "American Hegemony Comes Home: The Chilean Laboratory and the Neoliberalization of the United States." *Alternatives: Global, Local, Political* 38 (2): 103–21.

Barkan, Elazar. 2011. "The Politics of Return: When Rights Become Rites." In *Rites of Return: Diaspora Poetics and the Politics of Memory*, edited by Marianne Hirsch and Nancy K. Miller, 227–38. New York: Columbia University Press.

Baroud, Ramzy. 2006. *The Second Palestinian Intifada: A Chronicle of a People's Struggle.* London: Pluto.

Basso, Keith H. 1996. *Wisdom Sits in Places: Landscape and Language among the Western Apache.* Albuquerque: University of New Mexico Press.

Bayat, Asef. 2003. "The 'Street' and the Politics of Dissent in the Arab World." *Middle East Report* 226:10–17.

——. 2013. *Life as Politics: How Ordinary People Change the Middle East*. 2nd ed. Stanford, CA: Stanford University Press.

Beaumont, Peter. 2015. "Israel Exonerates Itself over Gaza Beach Killings of Four Children Last Year." *Guardian*, June 11. https://www.theguardian.com/world/2015/jun/11/israel-clears-military-gaza-beach-children.

Bender, Barbara. 1993. "Introduction: Landscape—Meaning and Action." In *Landscape: Politics and Perspectives*, edited by Barbara Bender, 1–17. Oxford: Berg.

——. 2001. Introduction to *Contested Landscapes: Movement, Exile and Place*, edited by Barbara Bender and Margot Winer, 1–18. Oxford: Berg.

Bilbija, Ksenija, and Leigh A. Payne, eds. 2011. *Accounting for Violence: Marketing Memory in Latin America*. Durham, NC: Duke University Press.

Bille, Mikkel, Frida Hastrup, and Tim Flohr Sørensen. 2010. "Introduction: An Anthropology of Absence." In *An Anthropology of Absence: Materializations of Transcendence and Loss*, edited by Mikkel Bille, Frida Hastrup, and Tim Flohr Sørensen, 3–22. London: Springer.

Bishop, Karen Elizabeth. 2014. "The Architectural History of Disappearance: Rebuilding Memory Sites in the Southern Cone." *Journal of the Society of Architectural Historians* 73 (4): 556–78.

Bowman, Glenn. 1988. "Tales of the Lost Land: Palestinian Identity and the Formation of Nationalist Consciousness." *New Formations* 5:31–52.

——. 2004. "About a Wall." *Social Analysis* 48 (1): 149–55.

Boyarin, Jonathan. 1994. "Space, Time, and the Politics of Memory." In *Remapping Memory: The Politics of TimeSpace*, edited by Jonathan Boyarin, 1–38. Minneapolis: University of Minnesota Press.

Brah, Avtar. 1996. *Cartographies of Diaspora: Contesting Identities*. London: Routledge.

Brand, Laurie. 1988. "Palestinians in Syria: The Politics of Integration." *Middle East Journal* 42 (4): 621–63.

Bray, Donald W. 1962. "The Political Emergence of Arab-Chileans, 1952–1958." *Journal of Inter-American Studies* 4 (4): 557–62.

Brender, Valerie. 2010. "Economic Transformations in Chile: The Formation of the Chicago Boys." *American Economist* 55 (1): 111–22.

Bröning, Michael. 2011. *The Politics of Change in Palestine: State-Building and Non-violent Resistance*. London: Pluto.

Brubaker, Rogers. 2005. "The 'Diaspora' Diaspora." *Ethnic and Racial Studies* 28 (1): 1–19.

Busse, Jan. 2015. "The Biopolitics of Statistics and Census in Palestine." *International Political Sociology* 9:70–89.

Butler, Judith. 2015. "Human Shield." London Review of International Law Annual Lecture, London School of Economics, February 4.

Cappelletto, Francesca. 2003. "Long-Term Memory of Extreme Events: From Autobiography to History." *Journal of the Royal Anthropological Institute* 9:241–60.

Carsten, Janet. 1995. "The Politics of Forgetting: Migration, Kinship and Memory on the Periphery of the Southeast Asian State." *Journal of the Royal Anthropological Institute* 1 (2): 317–35.

Casey, Edward S. 1997. *The Fate of Place: A Philosophical History*. Berkeley: University of California Press.

Chomsky, Noam. 2014. "The Real Reason Israel 'Mows the Lawn' in Gaza." AlterNet, September 9. http://www.alternet.org/noam-chomsky-real-reason-israel-mows-lawn-gaza.

Chovanec, Donna M., and Alexandra Benitez. 2008. "The Penguin Revolution in Chile: Exploring Intergenerational Learning in Social Movements." *Journal of Contemporary Issues in Education* 3 (1): 39–57.

Collier, Simon, and William F. Sater. 2004. *A History of Chile, 1808–2002.* 2nd ed. Cambridge: Cambridge University Press.

Collins, Cath. 2011. "The Moral Economy of Memory: Public and Private Commemorative Space in Post-Pinochet Chile." In *Accounting for Violence: Marketing Memory in Latin America*, edited by Ksenija Bilbija and Leigh A. Payne, 235–63. Durham, NC: Duke University Press.

Collins, John. 2004. *Occupied by Memory: The Intifada Generation and the Palestinian State of Emergency.* New York: NYU Press.

Connerton, Paul. 1989. *How Societies Remember.* Cambridge: Cambridge University Press.

——. 2008. "Seven Types of Forgetting." *Memory Studies* 1 (1): 59–71.

——. 2009. *How Modernity Forgets.* Cambridge: Cambridge University Press.

Consejo de Monumentos Nacionales de Chile. 2016. "Consejo de Monumentos aprueba declaratoria como Monumento Histórico de Colonia Dignidad." Monumentos.cl, March 23. http://www.monumentos.cl/consejo/606/w3-article-56950.html.

Conte, Gonzalo. 2015. "A Topography of Memory: Reconstructing the Architectures of Terror in the Argentine Dictatorship." *Memory Studies* 8 (1): 86–101.

Corsín Jiménez, Alberto. 2003. "On Space as a Capacity." *Journal of the Royal Anthropological Institute* 9:137–53.

Crang, Mike, and Penny S. Travlou. 2001. "The City and Topologies of Memory." *Environment and Planning D: Society and Space* 19:161–77.

Cresswell, Tim. 1996. *In Place / Out of Place: Geography, Ideology, and Transgression.* Minneapolis: University of Minnesota Press.

Crow, Joanna. 2013. *The Mapuche in Modern Chile: A Cultural History.* Gainesville: University Press of Florida.

Crownshaw, Richard, Jane Kilby, and Antony Rowland, eds. 2010. *The Future of Memory.* New York: Berghahn Books.

Dalsgaard, Steffen, and Morten Nielsen. 2015. "Introduction: Time and the Field." In *Time and the Field*, edited by Steffen Dalsgaard and Morten Nielsen, 1–19. New York: Berghahn Books.

Darweish, Marwan, and Andrew Rigby. 2015. *Popular Protest in Palestine: The Uncertain Future of Unarmed Resistance.* London: Pluto.

Davis, Rochelle A. 2011. *Palestinian Village Histories: Geographies of the Displaced.* Stanford, CA: Stanford University Press.

De Cesari, Chiara, and Ann Rigney, eds. 2014. *Transnational Memory: Circulation, Articulation, Scales.* Berlin: De Gruyter.

Deleuze, Gilles, and Félix Guattari. (1988) 2004. *A Thousand Plateaus.* Translated by Brian Massumi. London: Continuum.

Dwyer, Owen J., and Derek H. Alderman. 2008. "Memorial Landscapes: Analytic Questions and Metaphors." *GeoJournal* 73 (3): 165–78.

Edensor, Tim. 2005. "The Ghosts of Industrial Ruins: Ordering and Disordering Memory in Excessive Space." *Environment and Planning D: Society and Space* 23:829–49.

——. 2008. "Mundane Hauntings: Commuting through the Phantasmagoric Working-Class Spaces of Manchester, England." *Cultural Geographies* 15:313–33.

Edkins, Jenny. 2003. *Trauma and the Memory of Politics.* Cambridge: Cambridge University Press.

El-Attar, Heba. 2011. "Palestinian and Jewish Communal Press in Chile: The Case of *Al-Damir* and *La Palabra Israelita*." *Latin American and Caribbean Ethnic Studies* 6 (2): 189–206.

El Ciudadano. 2015. "Segunda funa a Teatro Universidad de Chile por obra patrocinada por Embajada de Israel." July 12. http://www.elciudadano. cl/2015/07/12/187439/.

Elsey, Brenda. 2011. *Citizens and Sportsmen: Fútbol and Politics in Twentieth-Century Chile.* Austin: University of Texas Press.

Erekat, Noura, and Marc Lamont Hill. 2019. "Black-Palestinian Transnational Solidarity: Renewals, Returns, and Practice." *Journal of Palestine Studies* 48 (4): 7–16.

Erll, Astrid. 2011. "Travelling Memory." *Parallax* 17 (4): 4–18.

Escoffier, Simón. 2014. "The Dictatorship Has Not Ended: Chile's September Riots." *Open Democracy*, October 19. https://www.opendemocracy.net/sim% C3%B3n-escoffier/dictatorship-has-not-ended-chile%E2%80%99s- september-riots.

Fabian, Johannes. (1983) 2002. *Time and the Other: How Anthropology Makes Its Object.* New York: Columbia University Press.

——. 2010. "Ethnography and Memory." In *Ethnographic Practice in the Present*, edited by Marit Melhuus, Jon P. Mitchell, and Helena Wulff, 16–27. New York: Berghahn Books.

Falconer, Bruce. 2008. "The Torture Colony: In a Remote Part of Chile, an Evil German Evangelist Built a Utopia Whose Members Helped the Pinochet Regime Perform Its Foulest Deeds." *American Scholar* 77 (4): 33–53.

Feldman, Keith P. 2015. *A Shadow over Palestine: The Imperial Life of Race in America.* Minneapolis: University of Minnesota Press.

Fentress, James, and Chris Wickham, eds. 1992. *Social Memory.* Cambridge: Blackwell.

Foote, Kenneth E., and Maoz Azaryahu. 2007. "Toward a Geography of Memory: Geographical Dimensions of Public Memory." *Journal of Political and Military Sociology* 35 (1): 125–44.

Foroohar, Manzar. 2011. "Palestinians in Central America: From Temporary Emigrants to a Permanent Diaspora." *Journal of Palestine Studies* 40 (3): 6–22.

Foucault, Michel. 1977. *Language, Counter Memory, Practice: Selected Essays and Interviews.* Translated by Donald F. Bouchard and Sherry Simon. Ithaca, NY: Cornell University Press.

——. 1986. "Of Other Spaces." Translated by Jay Miskowiec. *Diacritics* 16 (1): 22–27.

Frazier, Lessie Jo. 2007. *Salt in the Sand: Memory, Violence, and the Nation-State in Chile, 1890 to the Present.* Durham, NC: Duke University Press.

French, Brigittine M. 2012. "The Semiotics of Collective Memories." *Annual Review of Anthropology* 41:337–57.

Frens-String, Joshua. 2013. "A New Politics for a New Chile." *NACLA Report on the Americas* 46 (3): 28–33.

Garretón, Manuel Antonio. (1989) 2001. "Popular Mobilization and the Military Regime in Chile: The Complexities of the Invisible Transition." In *Power and Popular Protest: Latin American Social Movements*, edited by Susan Eckstein, 259–77. Berkeley: University of California Press.

Gillis, John R. 1994. "Memory and Identity: The History of a Relationship." In *Commemorations: The Politics of National Identity*, edited by John R. Gillis, 3–24. Princeton, NJ: Princeton University Press.

Goldenberg, Tia. 2015. "Growing BDS Movement Raises Alarm among Israeli Leaders." *Haaretz*, July 7. http://www.haaretz.com/news/middle-east/1.664833.

Gómez-Barris, Macarena. 2009. *Where Memory Dwells: Culture and State Violence in Chile*. Berkeley: University of California Press.

———. 2010. "Reinscribing Memory through the Other 9/11." In *Toward a Sociology of the Trace*, edited by Herman Gray and Macarena Gómez-Barris, 235–56. Minneapolis: University of Minnesota Press.

———. 2015. "Mapuche Mnemonics: Beyond Modernity's Violence." *Memory Studies* 8 (1): 75–85.

González, Nancie L. 1992. *Dollar, Dove, and Eagle: One Hundred Years of Palestinian Migration to Honduras*. Ann Arbor: University of Michigan Press.

Gould, Rebecca. 2014a. "Sumud: The Palestinian Art of Existence." *World Policy Journal*, Fall 2014: 99–106.

———. 2014b. "The Materiality of Resistance: Israel's Apartheid Wall in an Age of Globalization." *Social Text* 32 (1): 1–21.

Graeber, David. 2015. "Hostile Intelligence: Reflections from a Visit to the West Bank." *International Times*, July 30. http://internationaltimes.it/hostile-intelligence-reflections-from-a-visit-to-the-west-bank/.

Gray, Herman, and Macarena Gómez-Barris, eds. 2010. *Toward a Sociology of the Trace*. Minneapolis: University of Minnesota Press.

Green Rioja, Romina A. 2021. "Collective Trauma, Feminism and the Threads of Popular Power: A Personal and Political Account of Chile's 2019 Social Awakening." *Radical Americas* 6 (1).

Gregory, Derek. 1994. *Geographical Imaginations*. Cambridge: Blackwell.

Gren, Nina. 2015. "Being Home through Learning Palestinian Sociality: Swedish-Palestinian Houses in the West Bank." In *Diasporic Constructions of Home and Belonging*, edited by Florian Kläger and Klaus Stierstorfer, 229–48. Berlin: De Gruyter.

Guiskin, Maia. 2013. "Ser Judío en Chile: Identidad y conflicto palestino-israelí." Master's thesis, University of Chile.

Guzmán, Patricio, dir. 2010. *Nostalgia for the Light* [*Nostalgia de la Luz*]. DVD. Paris: Atacama Productions.

Guzman-Concha, Cesar. 2012. "The Students' Rebellion in Chile: Occupy Protest or Classic Social Movement?" *Social Movement Studies* 11 (3–4): 408–15.

Hadid, Diaa, and Marlise Simons. 2015. "Palestinians Join International Criminal Court, but Tread Cautiously at First." *New York Times*, April 1. http://www.nytimes.com/2015/04/02/world/middleeast/palestinians-join-international-criminal-court-but-tread-cautiously-at-first.html.

Hage, Ghassan. 2009. "Hating Israel in the Field: On Ethnography and Political Emotions." *Anthropological Theory* 9 (1): 59–79.

Halbwachs, Maurice. 1992. *On Collective Memory*. Edited and translated by Lewis A. Coser. Chicago: University of Chicago Press.

Hallward, Maia Carter. 2013. *Transnational Activism and the Israeli-Palestinian Conflict*. New York: Palgrave Macmillan.

Halper, Jeff. 2015. *War against the People: Israel, the Palestinians and Global Pacification*. London: Pluto.

Hammer, Juliane. 2005. *Palestinians Born in Exile: Diaspora and the Search for a Homeland*. Austin: University of Texas Press.

Han, Clara. 2012. *Life in Debt: Times of Care and Violence in Neoliberal Chile*. Berkeley: University of California Press.

Hanafi, Sari. 2005. "Reshaping Geography: Palestinian Community Networks in Europe and the New Media." *Journal of Ethnic and Migration Studies* 31 (3): 581–98.

——. 2012. "Explaining Spacio-cide in the Palestinian Territory: Colonization, Separation, and State of Exception." *Current* Sociology 61 (2): 190–205.

Harmer, Tanya. 2013. "Fractious Allies: Chile, the United States, and the Cold War, 1973–76." *Diplomatic History* 37 (1): 109–43.

Hass, Amira. 2011. "Between Two Returns." In *Rites of Return: Diaspora Poetics and the Politics of Memory*, edited by Marianne Hirsch and Nancy K. Miller, 173–84. New York: Columbia University Press.

Hayden, Patrick. 2014. "Systemic Evil and the International Political Imagination." *International Politics* 51 (4): 424–40.

Hénaff, Marcel, and Tracy B. Strong. 2001. "The Conditions of Public Space: Vision, Speech, and Theatricality." In *Public Space and Democracy*, edited by Marcel Hénaff and Tracy B. Strong, 1–32. Minneapolis: University of Minnesota Press.

Hiller, Harry H., and Tara M. Franz. 2004. "New Ties, Old Ties and Lost Ties: The Use of the Internet in Diaspora." *New Media and Society* 6 (6): 731–52.

Hirsch, Marianne. 1997. *Family Frames: Photography, Narrative, and Postmemory*. Cambridge, MA: Harvard University Press.

——. 2008. "The Generation of Postmemory." *Poetics Today* 29 (1): 103–28.

Hirsch, Marianne, and Nancy K. Miller. 2011. Preface to *Rites of Return: Diaspora Poetics and the Politics of Memory*, edited by Marianne Hirsch and Nancy K. Miller, xi–xiii. New York: Columbia University Press.

Hite, Katherine. 2012. *Politics and the Art of Commemoration: Memorials to Struggle in Latin America and Spain*. London: Routledge.

Hite, Katherine, Cath Collins, and Alfredo Joignant. 2013. "The Politics of Memory in Chile." In *The Politics of Memory in Chile: From Pinochet to Bachelet*, edited by Cath Collins, Katherine Hite, and Alfredo Joignant, 1–29. Boulder, CO: First Forum.

Hite, Katherine, and Jordi Huguet. 2016. "Guiding Light." *Guernica*, March 17. https://www.guernicamag.com/daily/katherine-hite-jordi-huguet-guiding-light/.

Hochberg, Gil Z. 2015. *Visual Occupations: Violence and Visibility in a Conflict Zone*. Durham, NC: Duke University Press.

Hoelscher, Steven, and Derek H. Alderman. 2004. "Memory and Place: Geographies of a Critical Relationship." *Social and Cultural Geography* 5 (3): 347–55.

Hou, Jeffrey. 2010. "(Not) Your Everyday Public Space." In *Insurgent Public Space: Guerrilla Urbanism and the Remaking of Contemporary Cities*, edited by Jeffrey Hou, 1–17. London: Routledge.

Huneeus, Carlos. 2007. *The Pinochet Regime*. Translated by Lake Sagaris. Boulder, CO: Lynne Rienner.

Huyssen, Andreas. 2003. *Present Pasts: Urban Palimpsests and the Politics of Memory*. Stanford, CA: Stanford University Press.

Ingold, Tim. 1993. "The Temporality of the Landscape." *World Archeology* 25 (2): 152–74.

Jadue, Daniel. 2014. *Palestina: Crónica de un asedio*. Santiago: Inmaterial Media.

Jayyusi, Lena. 2007. "Iterability, Cumulativity, and Presence: The Relational Figures of Palestinian Memory." In *Nakba: Palestine, 1948, and the Claims of Memory*, edited by Ahmad Sa'di and Lila Abu-Lughod, 107–33. New York: Columbia University Press.

Jelin, Elizabeth. 2003. *State Repression and the Labors of Memory*. Translated by Judy Rein and Marcial Godoy-Anativia. Minneapolis: University of Minnesota Press.

Johansson, Anna, and Stellan Vinthagen. 2015. "Dimensions of Everyday Resistance: The Palestinian *Sumûd*." *Journal of Political Power* 8 (1): 109–39.

Johnson, Nuala C. 2005. "Locating Memory: Tracing the Trajectories of Remembrance." *Practicing Historical Geography* 33:165–79.

Jones, Owain, and Joanne Garde-Hansen, eds. 2012. *Geography and Memory: Explorations in Identity, Place and Becoming*. Basingstoke, UK: Palgrave Macmillan.

Kaplan, Temma. 2004. *Taking Back the Streets: Women, Youth, and Direct Democracy*. Berkeley: University of California Press.

Kårtveit, Bård Helge. 2014. *Dilemmas of Attachment: Identity and Belonging among Palestinian Christians*. Leiden: Brill.

Kaschl, Elke. 2003. *Dance and Authenticity in Israel and Palestine: Performing the Nation*. Leiden: Brill.

Kelly, Tobias. 2009. "Returning to Palestine: Confinement and Displacement under Israeli Occupation." In *Struggles for Home: Violence, Hope and the Movement of People*, edited by Stef Jansen and Staffan Löfving, 25–41. New York: Berghahn Books.

Khalidi, Rashid. 2021. "What We're Seeing Now Is Just the Latest Chapter in Israel's Dispossession of the Palestinians." *Washington Post*, May 13. https://www.washingtonpost.com/opinions/2021/05/13/what-were-seeing-now-is-just-latest-chapter-israels-dispossession-palestinians/.

Khalidi, Walid, ed. 2006. *All That Remains: The Palestinian Villages Occupied and Depopulated by Israel in 1948*. Washington, DC: Institute for Palestine Studies.

Khalili, Laleh. 2005. "Virtual Nation: Palestinian Cyberculture in Lebanese Camps." In *Palestine, Israel, and the Politics of Popular Culture*, edited by Rebecca L. Stein and Ted Swedenburg, 126–49. Durham, NC: Duke University Press.

——. 2007. *Heroes and Martyrs of Palestine: The Politics of National Commemoration*. Cambridge: Cambridge University Press.

——. 2010. "Palestinians: The Politics of Control, Invisibility, and the Spectacle." In *Manifestations of Identity: The Lived Reality of Palestinian Refugees in Lebanon*, edited by Muhammad Ali Khalidi, 126–45. Beirut: Institute for Palestine Studies.

Khatib, Lina. 2012. *Image Politics in the Middle East: The Role of the Visual in Political Struggle*. London: I. B. Tauris.

Klep, Katrien. 2012. "Tracing Collective Memory: Chilean Truth Commissions and Memorial Sites." *Memory Studies* 5 (3): 259–69.

——. 2013. "Transitional Justice and Local Memory: Commemoration and Social Action in Londres 38, Especio de Memorias." In *Transitional Justice: Images and Memories*, edited by Chrisje Brants and Dina Siegel, 105–21. Farnham, UK: Ashgate.

Klich, Ignacio, and Jeffrey Lesser. 1996. "Introduction: 'Turco' Immigrants in Latin America." *Americas* 53 (1): 1–14.

——, eds. 1998. *Arab and Jewish Immigrants in Latin America: Images and Realities*. New York: Routledge.

Kornbluh, Peter. (2003) 2013. *The Pinochet File: A Declassified Dossier on Atrocity and Accountability*. New York: New Press.

Koselleck, Reinhart. 2004. *Futures Past: On the Semantics of Historical Time*. Translated by Keith Tribe. New York: Columbia University Press.

Kublitz, Anja. 2011. "The Sound of Silence: The Reproduction and Transformation of Global Conflicts within Palestinian Families in Denmark." In *Mobile Bodies, Mobile Souls: Family, Religion and Migration in a Global World*, edited by Mikkel Rytter and Karen Fog Olwig, 161–80. Aarhus: Aarhus University Press.

Lazar, Sian. 2014. "Historical Narrative, Mundane Political Time, and Revolutionary Moments: Coexisting Temporalities in the Lived Experience of Social Movements." *Journal of the Royal Anthropological Institute* 20 (April): 91–108.

Lazzara, Michael J., and Vicky Unruh, eds. 2009. *Telling Ruins in Latin America*. New York: Palgrave Macmillan.

Lefebvre, Henri. (1974) 1991. *The Production of Space*. Translated by Donald Nicholson-Smith. Malden, UK: Blackwell.

Lesser, Jeffrey, and Raanan Rein. 2011. Introduction to *Latin American and Caribbean Ethnic Studies* 6 (2): 115–19.

Lévy-Bruhl, Lucien. 1935. *Primitives and the Supernatural*. Translated by Lilian A. Clare. New York: E. P. Dutton.

Lira, Elizabeth. 2011. "Chile: Dilemmas of Memory." In *The Memory of State Terrorism in the Southern Cone*, edited by Francesca Lessa and Vincent Druliolle, 107–32. New York: Palgrave Macmillan.

Loveman, Brian, and Elizabeth Lira. 2007. "Truth, Justice, Reconciliation, and Impunity as Historical Themes: Chile, 1814–2006." *Radical History Review* 97:43–76.

Low, Setha M. 2009. "Towards an Anthropological Theory of Space and Place." *Semiotica* 175:21–37.

Lowenthal, David. 1999. Preface to *The Art of Forgetting*, edited by Adrian Forty and Susanne Küchler, xi–xiii. Oxford: Berg.

Lubin, Alex. 2014. *Geographies of Liberation: The Making of an Afro-Arab Political Imaginary*. Chapel Hill: University of North Carolina Press.

MacWilliam, Nick. 2014. "Chile's Support for Palestine: Two-Faced on Indigenous Rights." *Open Democracy*, August 12. https://www.opendemocracy.net/opensecurity/nick-macwilliam/chile's-support-for-palestine-twofaced-on-indigenous-rights.

Malpas, Jeff. (1999) 2004. *Place and Experience: A Philosophical Topography*. Cambridge: Cambridge University Press.

Márquez, Francisca. 2014. "Inmigrantes en territorios de frontera. La ciudad de los otros. Santiago de Chile." *EURE* 40 (120): 49–72.

Mason, Victoria. 2007. "Children of the 'Idea of Palestine': Negotiating Identity, Belonging and Home in the Palestinian Diaspora." *Journal of Intercultural Studies* 28 (3): 271–85.

Massad, Joseph. 2015. "The Cultural Work of Recovering Palestine." *boundary 2* 42 (4): 187–219.

Massey, Doreen. 1995. "Places and Their Pasts." *History Workshop Journal* 39:182–92.

———. 1999. "Space-Time, 'Science' and the Relationship between Physical Geography and Human Geography." *Transactions of the Institute of British Geographers* 24 (3): 261–76.

———. 2005. *For Space*. London: SAGE.

———. 2009. "Concepts of Space and Power in Theory and in Political Practice." *Documents d'Anàlisi Geogràfica* 55:15–26.

———. 2011. "Landscape/Space/Politics: An Essay." https://thefutureoflandscape.wordpress.com/landscapespacepolitics-an-essay/.

Mattar, Ahmad Hassan. 1941. *Guía social de la colonia árabe en Chile (Siria, Palestina, Libanesa)*. Santiago: Ahues Hermanos.

Maus, Gunnar. 2015. "Landscape of Memory: A Practice Theory Approach to Geographies of Memory." *Geographica Helvetica* 70:215–23.

Mavroudi, Elizabeth. 2008. "Palestinians in Diaspora, Empowerment and Informal Political Space." *Political Geography* (27): 57–73.

McFarlane, Colin. 2011. "Assemblage and Critical Urbanism." *City* 15 (2): 204–24.

Meade, Teresa. 2001. "Holding the Junta Accountable: Chile's 'Sitios de Memoria' and the History of Torture, Disappearance, and Death." *Radical History Review* 79:123–39.

Moulian, Tomás. 1997. *Chile actual: Anatomía de un mito.* Santiago: LOM Ediciones.

Munn, Nancy D. 1992. "The Cultural Anthropology of Time: A Critical Essay." *Annual Review of Anthropology* 21:93–123.

Murphy, Kaitlin M. 2019. *Mapping Memory: Visuality, Affect, and Embodied Politics in the Americas.* New York: Fordham University Press.

Naguib, Nefissa. 2008. "Storytelling: Armenian Family Albums in the Diaspora." *Visual Anthropology* 21:231–44.

Navaro-Yashin, Yael. 2012. *The Make-Believe Space: Affective Geography in a Postwar Polity.* Durham, NC: Duke University Press.

Nora, Pierre. 1989. "Between Memory and History: *Les Lieux de Mémoire.*" *Representations* 26:7–24.

Norman, Julie M. 2010. *The Second Palestinian Intifada: Civil Resistance.* London: Routledge.

Olick, Jeffrey K., and Joyce Robbins. 1998. "Social Memory Studies: From 'Collective Memory' to the Historical Sociology of Mnemonic Practices." *Annual Review of Sociology* 24:105–40.

Pacheco, Juan Antonio. 2006. "La prensa árabe en Chile: Sueños y realidades árabes en un mundo nuevo." *MEAH* 55:277–322.

Paley, Julia. 2001. *Marketing Democracy: Power and Social Movements in Post-Dictatorship Chile.* Berkeley: University of California Press.

Pappé, Ilan. 2006. *The Ethnic Cleansing of Palestine.* London: Oneworld.

Parkinson, John R. 2012. *Democracy and Public Space: The Physical Sites of Democratic Performance.* Oxford: Oxford University Press.

Pearlman, Wendy. 2011. *Violence, Nonviolence, and the Palestinian National Movement.* New York: Cambridge University Press.

Peteet, Julie. 2005. *Landscape of Hope and Despair: Palestinian Refugee Camps.* Philadelphia: University of Pennsylvania Press.

——. 2008. "Stealing Time." *Middle East Report* 248:14–15.

——. 2017. *Space and Mobility in Palestine.* Bloomington: Indiana University Press.

Power, Margaret. 2002. *Right-Wing Women in Chile: Feminine Power and the Struggle against Allende 1964–1973.* University Park: Pennsylvania State University Press.

——. 2004. "More Than Mere Pawns: Right-Wing Women in Chile." *Journal of Women's History* 16 (3): 138–51.

Rebolledo Hernández, Antonia. 1994. "La 'Turcofobia': Discriminación antiárabe en Chile, 1900–1950." *Historia* 28:249–72.

Richard, Nelly. 2009. "Sites of Memory, Emptying Remembrance." In *Telling Ruins in Latin America,* edited by Michael J. Lazzara and Vicky Unruh, 175–82. New York: Palgrave Macmillan.

Richter-Devroe, Sophie. 2013. "'Like Something Sacred': Palestinian Refugees' Narratives on the Right of Return." *Refugee Survey Quarterly* 32 (2): 92–115.

Rigby, Andrew. 2015. *The First Palestinian Intifada Revisited.* Ed, Sweden: Irene.

Roberts, Kenneth M. 2012. "Market Reform, Programmatic (De)alignment, and Party System Stability in Latin America." *Comparative Political Studies* 46 (11): 1422–52.

Rothberg, Michael. 2009. *Multidirectional Memory: Remembering the Holocaust in the Age of Decolonization.* Stanford, CA: Stanford University Press.

——. 2014. "Afterword: Locating Transnational Memory." *European Review* 22 (4): 652–56.

Runia, Eelco. 2006. "Presence." *History and Theory* 45:1–29.

Ryan, Caitlin. 2016. *Bodies, Power, and Resistance in the Middle East: Experiences of Subjectification in the Occupied Palestinian Territories.* New York: Routledge.

Sa'di, Ahmad H., and Lila Abu-Lughod, eds. 2007. *Nakba: Palestine, 1948, and the Claims of Memory.* New York: Columbia University Press.

Said, Edward. 1978. *Orientalism.* New York: Vintage Books.

——. 1999. *Out of Place: A Memoir.* London: Granta Books.

——. 2000. "Invention, Memory, and Place." *Critical Inquiry* 26 (2): 175–92.

Salamanca, Omar Jabary, Mezna Qato, Kareem Rabie, and Sobhi Samour. 2012. "Past Is Present: Settler Colonialism in Palestine." *Settler Colonial Studies* 2 (1): 1–8.

Saona, Margarita. 2014. *Memory Matters in Transitional Peru.* New York: Palgrave Macmillan.

Sayegh [Sayigh], Rosemary. 2013. "Palestinian Refugee Identity/ies: Generation, Region, Class." In *Palestinian Refugees: Different Generations, but One Identity,* edited by Sunaina Miari, 13–28. Birzeit: Ibrahim Abu-Lughod Institute of International Studies, Birzeit University.

Sayigh, Rosemary. (1979) 2007. *The Palestinians: From Peasants to Revolutionaries.* London: Zed Books.

Schiocchet, Leonardo. 2013. "Palestinian Sumud: Steadfastness, Ritual, and Time among Palestinian Refugees." In *Palestinian Refugees: Different Generations, but One Identity,* edited by Sunaina Miari, 67–90. Birzeit: Ibrahim Abu-Lughod Institute of International Studies, Birzeit University.

Schulz, Helena Lindholm. 2003. *The Palestinian Diaspora: Formation of Identities and Politics of Homeland.* London: Routledge.

Schwabe, Siri. 2017. "A Struggle for Space (Elsewhere): Marching for Gaza in Santiago de Chile." In *Spatial Justice and Diaspora,* edited by Sarah Keenan and Emma Patchett, 51–63. Oxford: Counterpress.

——. 2018a. "Paradoxes of Erasure: Palestinian Memory and the Politics of Forgetting in Post-dictatorship Chile." *Interventions* 20 (5): 651–65.

——. 2018b. "Resistance in Representation: The Diasporic Politics of Club Deportivo Palestino." *Soccer & Society* 20 (4): 693–703.

——. 2021. "A Heritage of Otherness: Memory Haunts and Urban Development on the 'Other Side' of Santiago de Chile." *Ethnos.* https://doi.org/10.1080/00141844 .2021.1973057.

Sehnbruch, Kirsten, and Sofia Donoso. 2011. "Chilean Winter of Discontent: Are Protests Here to Stay?" *Open Democracy,* August 21. https://www. opendemocracy.net/kirsten-sehnbruch-sofia-donoso/chilean-winter-of-discontent-are-protests-here-to-stay.

Seikaly, Sherene. 2014. "Bodies and Needs: Lessons from Palestine." *International Journal of Middle East Studies* 46:784–86.

Selwyn, Tom. 2001. "Landscapes of Separation: Reflections on the Symbolism of By-Pass Roads in Palestine." In *Contested Landscapes: Movement, Exile and Place,* edited by Barbara Bender and Margot Winer, 225–40. Oxford: Berg.

Sen, Somdeep. 2020. *Decolonizing Palestine: Hamas between the Anticolonial and the Postcolonial.* Ithaca, NY: Cornell University Press.

Shaw, Rosalind, Lars Waldorf, and Pierre Hazan, eds. 2010. *Localizing Transitional Justice: Interventions and Priorities after Mass Violence.* Stanford, CA: Stanford University Press.

Shohat, Ella, and Evelyn Alsultany. 2013. "The Cultural Politics of 'the Middle East' in the Americas: An Introduction." In *Between the Middle East and the Americas: The Cultural Politics of Diaspora*, edited by Evelyn Alsultany and Ella Shohat, 3–41. Ann Arbor: University of Michigan Press.

Sjørslev, Inger. 2012. "The Material Subject as Political: Style and Pointing in Public Performance." *Anthropological Theory* 12 (2): 209–28.

Slyomovics, Susan. 1998. *The Object of Memory: Arab and Jew Narrate the Palestinian Village*. Philadelphia: University of Pennsylvania Press.

Sökefeld, Martin. 2006. "Mobilizing in Transnational Space: A Social Movement Approach to the Formation of Diaspora." *Global Networks* 6 (3): 265–84.

Sontag, Susan. 2003. *Regarding the Pain of Others*. London: Penguin.

Sorensen, Kristin. 2011. "Chilean Historical Memory, Media, and Discourses of Human Rights." In *Global Memoryscapes: Contesting Remembrance in a Transnational Age*, edited by Kendall R. Phillips and G. Mitchell Reyes, 159–72. Tuscaloosa: University of Alabama Press.

Soysal, Yasemin Nuhoglu. 2000. "Citizenship and Identity: Living in Diasporas in Post-War Europe?" *Ethnic and Racial Studies* 23 (1): 1–15.

Springer, Simon. 2010. "Public Space as Emancipation: Meditations on Anarchism, Radical Democracy, Neoliberalism and Violence." *Antipode* 43 (2): 525–62.

———. 2014. "Space, Time, and the Politics of Immanence." *Global Discourse* 4 (2–3): 159–62.

Stein, Rebecca L. 2008. *Itineraries in Conflict: Israelis, Palestinians, and the Political Lives of Tourism*. Durham, NC: Duke University Press.

Stein, Rebecca L., and Ted Swedenburg. 2005. "Introduction: Popular Culture, Transnationality, and Radical History." In *Palestine, Israel, and the Politics of Popular Culture*, edited by Rebecca L. Stein and Ted Swedenburg, 1–23. Durham, NC: Duke University Press.

———, eds. 2005. *Palestine, Israel, and the Politics of Popular Culture*. Durham, NC: Duke University Press.

Stern, Steve J. 2006. *Battling for Hearts and Minds: Memory Struggles in Pinochet's Chile, 1973–1988*. Durham, NC: Duke University Press.

———. 2010. *Reckoning with Pinochet. The Memory Question in Democratic Chile, 1989–2006*. Durham, NC: Duke University Press.

Stoler, Ann Laura. 2016. *Duress: Imperial Durabilities in Our Times*. Durham, NC: Duke University Press.

Swedenburg, Ted. 2003. *Memories of Revolt: The 1936–1939 Rebellion and the Palestinian National Past*. Fayetteville: University of Arkansas Press.

Tawil-Souri, Helga. 2012. "It's Still about the Power of Place." *Middle East Journal of Culture and Communications* 5:86–95.

Tawil-Souri, Helga, and Miriyam Aouragh. 2014. "Intifada 3.0? Cyber Colonialism and Palestinian Resistance." *Arab Studies Journal* 22 (1): 102–33.

Taylor, Diana. 2011. "Trauma as Durational Performance: A Return to Dark Sites." In *Rites of Return: Diaspora Poetics and the Politics of Memory*, edited by Marianne Hirsch and Nancy K. Miller, 268–79. New York: Columbia University Press.

Terdiman, Richard. 1993. *Present Past: Modernity and the Memory Crisis*. Ithaca, NY: Cornell University Press.

Thomas, Julian. 1993. "The Politics of Vision and the Archeologies of Landscape." In *Landscape: Politics and Perspectives*, edited by Barbara Bender, 19–48. Oxford: Berg.

Till, Karen E. 2003. "Places of Memory." In *A Companion to Political Geography*, edited by John Agnew, Katharyne Mitchell, and Gerard Toal, 289–301. London: Blackwell.

Tilley, Christopher. 1994. *A Phenomenology of Landscape: Places, Paths and Monuments*. Oxford: Berg.

Tilly, Charles. 1995. *Popular Contention in Great Britain, 1758–1834*. Cambridge, MA: Harvard University Press.

Tonkin, Elizabeth. 1992. *Narrating Our Pasts: The Social Construction of Oral History*. Cambridge: Cambridge University Press.

Torrejón Vasquez, Stefanie. 2011. "Inmigración Árabe en Chile 1890–1920: Reflexiones en torno a los Discursos de Nación, Raza e Identidas Chileno-Árabe." Master's thesis, University of Chile.

Trigg, Dylan. 2012. *The Memory of Place: A Phenomenology of the Uncanny*. Athens: Ohio University Press.

Trouillot, Michel-Rolph. 1995. *Silencing the Past: Power and the Production of History*. Boston: Beacon.

Turki, Fawaz. 1977. "The Future of a Past: Fragments from the Palestinian Dream." *Journal of Palestine Studies* 6 (3): 66–76.

Van Dijck, José. 2007. *Mediated Memories in the Digital Age*. Stanford, CA: Stanford University Press.

Vergunst, Jo, Andrew Whitehouse, Nicolas Ellison, and Arnar Árnason. 2012. "Introduction: Landscapes beyond Land." In *Landscapes beyond Land: Routes, Aesthetics, Narratives*, edited by Arnar Árnason, Nicolas Ellison, Jo Vergunst, and Andrew Whitehouse, 1–14. New York: Berghahn Books.

Villalobos-Ruminott, Sergio. 2012. "The Chilean Winter." *Radical Philosophy* 171:11–15.

Watson, Sophie. 2006. *City Publics: The (Dis)enchantments of Urban Encounters*. London: Routledge.

Westmoreland, Mark R., and Diana K. Allan. 2016. "Visual Revolutions in the Middle East." *Visual Anthropology* 29:205–10.

White, Ben. 2018. *Cracks in the Wall: Beyond Apartheid in Palestine/Israel*. London: Pluto.

Whitehead, Anne. 2009. *Memory*. London: Routledge.

Winn, Peter. 1986. *Weavers of Revolution: The Yarur Workers and Chile's Road to Socialism*. New York: Oxford University Press.

Winter, Jay. 1998. *Sites of Memory, Sites of Mourning: The Great War in European Cultural History*. Cambridge: Cambridge University Press.

Wood, Nancy. 1999. *Vectors of Memory: Legacies of Trauma in Postwar Europe*. Oxford: Berg.

Wyndham, Marivic, and Peter Read. 2012. "Filling the Void of Trapped Memories: The Liberation of a Pinochet Centre of Torture." *Journal of Iberian and Latin American Research* 18 (1): 41–54.

——. 2014. "The Disappearing Museum." *Rethinking History* 18 (2): 165–80.

Young, James E. 1993. *The Texture of Memory: Holocaust Memorials and Meaning*. New Haven, CT: Yale University Press.

Index

www.ingramcontent.com/pod-product-compliance
Lightning Source LLC
Chambersburg PA
CBHW022009240725
30101CB00027B/1127